Six-week Start-Up

A step-by-step programme for starting your business, making money, and achieving your goals!

Rhonda Abrams

with Guy Clapperton

CAPSTONE

First published in 2008 by Capstone Publishing Ltd. (a Wiley Company)
The Atrium, Southern Gate, Chichester, PO19 8SQ, UK.
www.wileyeurope.com

Email (for orders and customer service enquires): cs-books@wiley.co.uk

Other Wiley Editorial Offices
John Wiley & Sons Inc., 111 River Street, Hoboken, NJ 07030, USA
Jossey-Bass, 989 Market Street, San Francisco, CA 94103-1741, USA
Wiley-VCH Verlag GmbH, Boschstr. 12, D-69469 Weinheim, Germany
John Wiley & Sons Australia Ltd, 42 McDougall Street, Milton, Queensland 4064,
Australia
John Wiley & Sons (Asia) Pte Ltd, 2 Clementi Loop #02-01, Jin Xing Distripark,
Singapore 129809
John Wiley & Sons Canada Ltd, 22 Worcester Road, Etobicoke, Ontario, Canada M9W
1L1

Wiley also publishes its books in a variety of electronic formats. Some content that
appears in print may not be available in electronic books.

A catalogue record for this book is available from the British Library.

ISBN 13: 978-1-84112-805-4

Typeset by Sparks, Oxford – www.sparkspublishing.com
Printed and bound in Great Britain by TJ International Ltd, Padstow, Cornwall

Substantial discounts on bulk quantities of Capstone Books are available to corporations,
professional associations and other organizations. For details telephone
John Wiley & Sons on (+44) 1243-770441, fax (+44) 1243 770571 or email
corporatedevelopment@wiley.co.uk

Who this book is for

This book is a step-by-step guide for getting a successful business up and running fast. It covers all aspects of launching a business, from licences, to bookkeeping to marketing to setting up shop. Everything is presented in a step-by-step format with checklists, worksheets, and top-notch advice from one of America's most highly regarded business writers.

This book is for you if:

- You're currently in the process of starting your own business and want to get things done as efficiently as possible, yet still do them right.

- You want to make certain you take care of all the details of getting a business underway, organise the process, and get some good advice.

- You're going to start a business soon and need a plan on how to go about it.

- You have an idea for a business but don't know where to start.

- You already run a business but would like to improve operations, marketing, and/or take care of essential aspects of growing a company.

- You're a student in an entrepreneurship or small business class and need to launch a complete business in a limited time period.

You probably do not need this book if:

- You've been in business many years, and you're not expanding or changing your business significantly.

- You've started many businesses successfully before and are starting another one; while this book may be a good organising tool, it's likely to cover information you've already learned from experience.

- You have no idea whatsoever of what business you want to start. If that's the case, the book you need is *What Business Should I Start?* also by The Planning Shop.

About the authors

Rhonda Abrams is a syndicated columnist, best-selling author, and popular public speaker. She has spent more than fifteen years advising, mentoring, and consulting with entrepreneurs and small business owners. Her knowledge of the small business market and her passion for entrepreneurship have made her one of the USA's most recognised advocates for small business.

An experienced entrepreneur, Rhonda has started three successful companies, including a small business planning consulting firm. Her experience gives her a strong real-life understanding of the challenges facing entrepreneurs. Currently, she is the founder and CEO of The Planning Shop, a company focused on providing entrepreneurs with high-quality information and tools for developing successful businesses.

Guy Clapperton contributed regularly to the Guardian's Business Sense section for small businesses throughout its eight-year run as columnist, editorial associate and podcaster. Before this he ran a newsletter focusing on small business issues and continues to be fascinated by entrepreneurialism.

Currently, Guy writes business articles for the Guardian, Financial Times, Esquire and numerous other publications. He also writes for the Times, Sunday Times, Mail on Sunday, Radio Times and other national publications. He broadcasts occasionally for BBC Radio London and the BBC World Service, normally about technology.

How to use this book

This book outlines a programme for you to get your business up and running quickly and successfully.

The Six-Week Start-Up Programme breaks down the many tasks of launching a business into six, manageable weeks. During each week, you'll focus on just a few major issues; this makes it possible for you to manage the necessary details without feeling overwhelmed.

Each week consists of:

- **Main accomplishments:** These are the major issues you have to deal with when you start your business, such as money, laws and regulations, operations. In order to help you stay focused and deal with these big issues efficiently, almost all of the tasks relating to the same major issue are handled in the same week.

- **Tasks:** Each accomplishment is then broken down into a series of tasks. This makes it easier for you to tackle the specific aspects of a major issue one-by-one. Check the box next to each task as you complete it.

- **Worksheets, checklists, planning forms:** To make completing your tasks easier, each week includes many helpful worksheets and planning forms. Use these to guide you as you go along. You may want to keep these completed forms even after you've opened your business to refer to from time-to-time.

- **Make appointments with:** Each week includes a suggestion of the appropriate experts or advisors who can help you complete that week's accomplishments and tasks.

These accomplishments and tasks have been arranged in a logical, efficient order, based on the real-life patterns and needs of entrepreneurs. Of course, this doesn't mean you have to follow these tasks in exactly this order—or that you have to complete all of them in just six weeks.

You can undertake these accomplishments in any order—or break up tasks into separate weeks!

In addition, throughout this book, you will find:

- **Questions to Ask:** Lists of suggested issues to deal with when you meet with other key contacts, such as investors, lawyers, accountants, and many more.

- **Red Tape Alerts:** To give you a "heads-up" warning when an issue may have legal or tax consequences.

- **What Would Rhonda Do:** Some insight and advice based on real-life experience.

- **Hot Links:** To help you find useful information and resources on the Internet quickly.

Use the Six-Week Start-Up Programme as a guide; it is not meant to be restrictive. If it takes you six months instead of six weeks, don't worry. Follow the pace that suits you. On the other hand, it's also possible to start making sales even before you've finished all aspects of this programme.

The important thing is to start! The best place to begin is right at the beginning—Week One!

Table of Contents

Who this book is for. iii

About the authors v

How to use this book vii

Introduction xv

WEEK 1: LAY THE FOUNDATION. 1

Clarify your business concept 5

- Identify your personal goals 7
- Spell out your business values. 9
- Remind yourself of your source of inspiration 12
- Describe your business concept 15
- Identify your strategic position 17
- Decide whether you want partners 18
- Decide whether you want investors 21
- Consider potential exit strategies. 22
- Discuss the impact of starting a business with your family 24
- Get some advice 25

Create your company identity. 26

- Choose a name 27
- Check out trademarks. 31
- Secure a domain name. 34
- Consider logos, straplines, and colours. 35
- Meet with a graphic designer. 39

Get organised 41
- Set up physical files 41
- Set up computer files 43
- Set up a contact management system 43
- Keep track of your company's vital statistics.................... 44
- Keep track of expenses... 45

WEEK 2: GET THE INFORMATION YOU NEED 47
Learn more about your industry................................... 50
- Make a list of your research questions 50
- Contact your industry association(s) 51
- Do online research.. 54
Research your target market 56
- Define your target market...................................... 59
- Determine if there are enough customers...................... 60
Check out your competition..................................... 62
- Identify your competitors 62
- Analyze your competition 63
- Compare competitors' pricing 67
Find suppliers... 68
Consider strategic partners...................................... 71
Broaden/establish your network 72
- Attend an entrepreneur or industry organisation meeting...... 76

WEEK 3: CUT THROUGH RED TAPE 79
Deal with legal and licensing matters............................ 82
- Choose a legal form and ownership structure 83
- Discuss ownership of your company............................ 86
- Apply for business licenses, permits, and ID numbers........... 90
- Registering for VAT.. 94
- Draw up basic contracts and other legal agreements 96
- Protect your intellectual property............................... 96
Build your team and personnel structure........................ 100
- Consider your support structure............................... 100
- Decide who you need on your team 103
- Examine the use of independent contractors................... 106
- Understand employment laws & consider personnel policies .. 109
- Appraise your management style............................... 117

WEEK 4: TAKE CARE OF OPERATIONS 123
Find and secure a location..................................... 126
Option 1: Rent space 127
- Decide on the necessary attributes of your location 127
- Meet with a real estate agent.................................. 131

- Compare properties..131
- Consider whether you need more than one location 133
Option 2: Set up a home office 135
- Find the space to work 135
- Figure out your phone, fax, and Internet connections 136
- Plan how to meet with customers 137
- Decide whether you need a separate business address........138
- Understand home-based office tax deductions 138
- Plan ways to separate work life from home life 140
- Deal with kids and pets 142
Option 3: Set up an "office" in your vehicle........................144
Design your work space and production process 145
- Design your layout...145
- Design your production process............................148
- Order/install utilities and facility improvements 150
- Order furniture and equipment.............................151
- Order inventory and/or raw materials.......................157
Research and purchase computers and other technology 159
- Develop an approach to buying technology 159
- Choose a phone system 161
- Choose software 163
- Choose hardware 164
- Get online 168
- Find ways to get technical help.............................173
Consider how you will distribute your products 174
Design procedures for handling administrative tasks............178
Deal with insurance 181
WEEK 5: DEAL WITH MONEY ISSUES 187
Deal with money matters..190
- Meet with an accountant 190
- Learn the lingo..191
- Take stock of your personal financial situation.................193
- Clean up your credit 195
- Set up your books..198
- Establish your prices 199
- Open a bank account 202
- Consider accepting credit cards 203
- Prepare simple financial forecasts..........................206
- Learn about taxes 208
Consider financing 216
- Determine whose money you want...........................218

- Develop a business plan 224

WEEK SIX: OPEN YOUR DOORS **227**

Develop a marketing plan **230**
- Clarify your company's message 230
- Come up with your Elevator Pitch 232
- Decide on marketing vehicles 236

Set up a simple website **251**
Start making sales! **255**
Hold your grand opening **270**
Look towards the future **271**
Index **277**

Worksheets

Goals for Starting My Business 4
My Personal Goals: The Four C's 6
My Business Values 10
My Role Models 11
My "Bright Idea" 13
My Business Concept 14
Basic Business Description 16
Discussing Partnership Terms 20
Business Name Comparison Chart 28
Creating My Identity 38
My Research Questions 52
Research Sources 55
Who are My Customers? 57
My Customer Profile 58
Size of My Market 61
My Competitors 64
Competitors' Price Comparison Chart 65
Potential Strategic Partners 70
Organisations to Join 74
Forms of Business Organisation Compared 84
People You've Given or Promised Stock 88
Stock Distribution Plan 89
Business Licenses & Permits 91
Vital Statistics 93
My Support System 101
Who Do I Need on My Team? 104
My Personnel Policies 110

Recruiting Employees 113
My Leadership Skills. 119
Things to Consider when Renting Space 128
Location/Space Comparison Chart. 132
Mobile Office Plan 143
Floor Plan Layout 146
Designing My Production Process 147
Office Move-in Checklist 149
Furniture Shopping List 152
Equipment Shopping List 153
Warranties and Service Contracts. 155
Supplier Comparison Chart. 158
My Phone Needs. 162
My Hardware Needs. 165
My Software Needs 166
Comparison Chart: Internet Hosting Companies 169
Distribution Agreement. 175
Retailer Comparison Chart 177
Comparison Chart: Insurance Coverage. 183
Taking Stock: What are My Existing Assets?. 194
My Credit Cards. 197
Comparison Chart: Banks. 204
Sales Projections. 210
Marketing Budget. 211
Profit & Loss Projection. 212
Cash Flow Projection. 214
My Tax Deadlines 217
Comparison Chart: Investors 220
My Elevator Pitch 233
Marketing Vehicles Comparison Chart 234
My Printing Needs 237
Trade Shows and Industry Events. 239
Getting Publicity. 242
Media Contacts 243
My Website Checklist. 253
My Sales Pitch 256

Introduction

In six weeks you can change your life!

Where are you going to be six weeks from today?

Six weeks from today, you can have your own business up-and-running, and you can be on the road to success.

You've had the dream of owning your business for some time; you even have an idea for your business concept. Now, I'm giving you the blueprint.

I'm going to help you get all the nitty-gritty details of starting a business out of the way so you can spend your time on things you really want to do—make your products, provide your service, be creative, make money, have fun!

With checklists and very specific advice, this book walks you through the process of starting your business, step-by-step. I've detailed the critical components of getting a business—a successful business—underway and created an easy-to-follow programme for dealing with those components.

Starting a business can seem overwhelming—there's so much to do, so much to figure out. How do you set prices? What licenses do you need?

How do you choose a location? Where do you find customers? Where do you get the money?

All these details seem paralyzing.

I know, because I've been there. I've started and built three successful companies. I still remember my first weeks in business—deciding on a business name, getting my first business card designed, figuring out a way to land my first customer. I was flustered by buying my first computer and struggled to learn my first computer program.

I wanted to make it easier—much easier—for you. And I wanted to not only deal with all those details, but I wanted to make sure you had some fun along the way—staying motivated and getting energised.

So, in this book, I've organised the start-up process into a comprehensive programme.

Each week, you'll see your:

- **Major accomplishments:** You'll be able to track your progress as you handle major components of starting a business

- **Tasks:** Each accomplishment is broken down into specific steps, making it easier and faster for you to achieve those accomplishments.

- **Appointments to make:** You'll quickly see what experts or authorities you need to make appointments with, speeding your startup process.

Using it:

- You'll understand and learn how to deal with the nitty-gritty details of starting a business.

- You'll be given the questions when you meet with others, such as lawyers, accountants, even prospective partners or investors.

- You'll discover additional sources and resources of business information, making your business start-up process less expensive and more effective.

- You'll learn which stuff you don't have to do—at least now—saving you valuable time.

- You'll get real-life advice.

This book covers everything from taxes to trade shows, accounting to advertising, customers to computers.

Of course, you might want to—or need to—take more than six weeks to get your own business underway. That's okay. Set your own pace. This book still serves as a plan—a "cookbook"—outlining the steps to launching your business—whether you take six weeks or six months.

Can I guarantee that in six weeks you'll be sitting on a beach counting your money? No. This isn't some get-rich-quick scheme.

Instead, this is a realistic, do-able, guide to getting your own business up-and-running.

If what's been holding you back from getting your business started is that you don't know where to start, or you're overwhelmed by the details, or you're afraid you don't have the money to pay for the advice you need, then this book is for you.

Where are you going to be six weeks from now?

week 1

LAY THE FOUNDATION

Main accomplishments:
- ✓ Clarify your business vision and concept
- ✓ Create your business identity
- ✓ Get organised

Make appointments with:
- ✓ Graphic Designer
- ✓ SBDC Counsellor

lay the fou

dation...

Congratulations! You're now officially starting your new business. During this first week, you're going to jump right in with some of the fun stuff of starting a business—like choosing a business name and developing a corporate identity—but most of the week is devoted to establishing a strong foundation for your new company: making sure your business concept is solid, developing a network of advisors and supporters to help you build and grow your company, and taking care of the organisational details to make day-to-day business life more effective and efficient.

In other words, we're going to make sure you get off to the right start.

Even if you are starting a one-person business, you're going to find it beneficial to develop a network of colleagues and associates, referral sources and supporters. No one succeeds alone—so right from Week One, you're going to start building your network.

GOALS FOR STARTING MY BUSINESS

Specific Goals:

Enter the number or amount you hope to achieve for your business in one year, five years, and ten years.

	One Year	Five Years	Ten Years
Number of Employees	_____	_____	_____
Number of Locations	_____	_____	_____
Annual Sales	_____	_____	_____
Profits or Profit Margin	_____	_____	_____
Number of Products/Services	_____	_____	_____
Awards/Recognition Received	_____	_____	_____
Ownership Allocation	_____	_____	_____
Other:	_____	_____	_____
_____	_____	_____	_____
_____	_____	_____	_____
_____	_____	_____	_____

Priorities:

Rate your priorities for your business.

	Urgent	Important	I'll get to it sooner or later	Not on the radar screen	Not applicable to my business
Add Employees	☐	☐	☐	☐	☐
Add New Lines	☐	☐	☐	☐	☐
Increase Marketing	☐	☐	☐	☐	☐
Add Locations	☐	☐	☐	☐	☐
Add Capacity	☐	☐	☐	☐	☐
Increase Salaries	☐	☐	☐	☐	☐
Increase Inventory	☐	☐	☐	☐	☐
Increase Profits	☐	☐	☐	☐	☐
Pay Debts	☐	☐	☐	☐	☐
Increase Reserve	☐	☐	☐	☐	☐
Acquire Other Companies	☐	☐	☐	☐	☐
Other:					
_____	☐	☐	☐	☐	☐
_____	☐	☐	☐	☐	☐
_____	☐	☐	☐	☐	☐
_____	☐	☐	☐	☐	☐

ACCOMPLISHMENT #1:
Clarify your business concept

Tasks:

- [ ] 1. Identify your personal goals
- [ ] 2. Spell out your business values
- [ ] 3. Remind yourself of your source of inspiration
- [ ] 4. Describe your business concept
- [ ] 5. Identify your strategic position
- [ ] 6. Decide whether you want partners
- [ ] 7. Decide whether you want investors
- [ ] 8. Consider potential exit strategies
- [ ] 9. Discuss the impact of starting a business with your family

If you were building a house, before you drew up the blueprints, laid the foundation, or even bought the land, you'd first have a vision of what you'd want that house to be: big or small, one story or two, in the city or in the country. You'd have a "vision" of your future home. The same is true when building a company: you need a vision of what you hope you'll achieve.

When you imagine your business, what do you hope for? To make a lot of money? Use your creativity? Have more flexibility in your life? Do you see yourself working alone or building a company with employees? Do you hope your company grows very large or do you want it to stay small?

As you launch your new company, it's important to clarify and evaluate your business concept. What is your long-term vision? What are your personal goals? What do you see as the business opportunity? From that, how do you define your business specifics—what it does, who it serves, how it differs from the competition?

Some entrepreneurs describe themselves as "visionaries" because they can conceive of grand schemes or bold new inventions. They envision their companies clobbering the competition, defining new product categories, perhaps growing to hundreds of millions—if not billions—of pounds.

MY PERSONAL GOALS: THE FOUR C'S

Make copies of this worksheet for yourself and your partners or key employees, if any.
Check the level of importance to you in each area.

	Extremely Important	Somewhat Important	Somewhat Unimportant	Not Important
Creativity				
Determining the design or look of products/packaging				
Creating new products or services				
Devising new business procedures/policies				
Identifying new company opportunities				
Creating new business materials				
Devising new ways of doing "old" things				
Other:				
Control				
Over own work responsibilities				
Over own time, work hours, etc.				
Over company decisions and directions				
Over products/services				
Over other employees				
Over work environment				
Over social/environmental impact of products/services				
Over own future and business' future				
Other:				
Challenge				
Long-term problem solving				
Critical problem solving (putting out fires)				
Handling many issues at one time				
Continually dealing with new issues				
Perfecting solutions, products or services				
Organising diverse projects and keeping the group goal-focuses				
Other:				

Cash

List approximate pound ranges for the following. Measure wealth as the value of stocks or of the company.

Income needed currently _____   Wealth desired in 2–5 years _____

Income desired in 12–24 months _____   Wealth desired in 6–10 years _____

Income desired in 2–5 years _____   Wealth desired 10+ years _____

But a business "vision" doesn't have to be revolutionary. The important part is that you identify what you see your business becoming: what it will do or make, how it will grow and compete, how big it will get.

Over time, your business vision will almost certainly change. As you gain experience and confidence, you may change the nature of your products or services, your personal goals may evolve, and the things that seem most important to you now may be much less so in the next few years.

Nevertheless, clarifying your current business vision and articulating your specific business concept gives you a stronger start as you begin building your company. Use the "Goals for Starting My Business" worksheet on page four as a starting place for defining your business goals.

1. Identify your personal goals

What are your personal goals in growing your business? Some businesses fail, and others flounder, because their founders or executives are uncertain what they really want to achieve, and they don't structure the company and their responsibilities in ways that satisfy their personal needs and ambitions.

The Four C's

For most entrepreneurs, their personal goals can be summed up by the Four C's: Creativity, Control, Challenge, and Cash. Of course, we each want all four of these to some degree, but knowing which we most want or need can help us structure our companies to best achieve our goals.

For instance, my very first clients were the owners of a small sportswear apparel company. The woman began the business because she was good at—and loved—designing clothes. Her primary motivation was being able to act on her creativity. But an apparel company doesn't run on designs alone. There are a myriad of purely "business" aspects of the company—sales, operations, manufacturing, etc. If she hadn't planned for it, she might have spent the majority of her time on such issues instead of designing. Fortunately, she had a partner to take over those responsibilities. She gave up some control—which wasn't a major concern of hers—to maintain her creativity.

Which of the Four C's motivates you most?

■ **Creativity.** Entrepreneurs want to leave their mark. Their companies are not only a means of making a living, but a way of creating something that bears their stamp. Creativity comes in many forms, from designing a new "thing," to devising a new business process, or even a new way to make sales, handle customers, or reward employees.

If you have a high need for creativity, make certain you remain involved in the creative process as your company develops. You'll want to shape your business so it's not just an instrument for earning an income but also a way for maintaining your creative stimulation and making a larger contribution to society. But don't overpersonalise your company, especially if it's large. Allow room for others, particularly partners and key personnel, to share in the creative process.

- **Control**. Most of us start businesses because we want more control over our own lives. Perhaps we want more control over how our good ideas are implemented. Perhaps we want, or need, more control of our work hours or conditions so we can be more involved in family, community, or even golf! Control is a major motivator for most entrepreneurs—usually more important than money. But how much control you need—especially on a day-to-day basis—directly influences how large your company can be.

  If you need or want a great deal of control over your time, you'll most likely need to keep your company smaller. In a large company, you have less immediate control over many decisions. If you're a person who needs control, you can still grow your business larger. You'll need to structure communication and reporting systems to ensure that you have sufficient information about and direction over developments to give you personal satisfaction. If you seek outside funding in the form of investors, understand the nature of control your funders will have and be certain you are comfortable with these arrangements.

- **Challenge.** If you're starting or expanding a business, it's clear you like challenge—at least to some degree. You're likely to be a problem-solver and risk-taker, enjoying the task of figuring out solutions to problems or devising new undertakings. Challenge-hungry entrepreneurs can be some of the most successful businesspeople, but they can also be their own worst enemies—flitting from one thing to another, never focusing long enough to succeed.

  If you have a high need for challenge in your business life, it's important to develop positive means to meet this need, especially once your company is established and the initial challenge of starting a company is met. Otherwise, you may find yourself continually starting new projects that divert attention from your company's main goals. As you plan your company, establish goals that not only provide you with sufficient stimulation, but also advance—rather than distract from—the growth of your business. (Or take up sky diving on the side!)

■ **Cash.** Every entrepreneur wants to make money. Perhaps it's just enough money to provide a decent income; perhaps it's so much money you can buy a jet. How much you want or need affects how you'll develop your business. Will you need investors and when? Will you sacrifice control to grow the business quickly?

Keep in mind there are sometimes trade-offs between personal goals: wanting more cash often means having less control; staying at the center of the creative process may mean you need to have a partner or grow slowly, once again trading off control or cash. Examine your personal goals and those of key personnel using "The Four C's" worksheet on page six.

2. Spell out your business values

As we build our companies, we have goals not only for what our business will help us achieve for ourselves, but also how our business will impact others: our employees, customers, the environment, our communities.

For many entrepreneurs, the business values they want their company to project are part of their inspiration for getting started in the first place.

Incorporating your values into your business will help you build a company that gives you greater satisfaction in the long term, and quite possibly, a more successful company as well. Having a company that ascribes to and practices certain positive values can be a competitive advantage in attracting and retaining employees and developing customer loyalty.

Be cautious, however, that as you build your business around your values, you do not impose your personal beliefs (especially religious or political beliefs) on others.

To help clarify the values you'd like to incorporate into your business, use the "My Business Values" worksheet on the next page.

MY BUSINESS VALUES

Describe what values are important to you in building your company as they relate to:

Corporate culture and nature of the work environment (management/employee relations and communication, work hours and flexibility, dress code, office location, décor, etc.):

Business Ethics (customer treatment; relations with vendors, distributors, competitors; advertising, etc.):

Employee Treatment (wages and benefits, lay-off policies, promotions, empowerment, etc):

Community and Civic Involvement:

The Environment:

Other:

MY ROLE MODELS

Use this space to list the names of people you admire, whether they're in business or not.

Name and Job or Role	What traits of theirs do you admire?	How could you incorporate those traits in your business?

3. Remind yourself of your source of inspiration

At some point in their business lives, all entrepreneurs are inspired—by an idea, a person, or an opportunity. That inspiration not only gets you started; it also keeps you going. You may reach a point down the road when you ask yourself, "Why did I start all this?" Re-read what you've written here when you need to be "re-inspired," or just to get a reminder of what your goals were from the beginning.

The worksheets in this section are also the starting point for articulating your business concept and identifying your niche and customer base.

My role models

Do you want to be another Richard Branson? Do you see yourself as a future Jonathan Ross? Or do you look up to your uncle who ran his own store or your older sister who has been self-employed for ten years?

Many of us are fortunate enough to have people in business whom we admire or would like to emulate. You may know them personally, or you may have read about their business practices or success.

Thinking about your role models can help you clarify your own business vision. If your business hero is Richard Branson, what is it about him that you admire? His ability to make a great deal of money? Build a huge business? His marketing and strategic capabilities? Or do you admire his technical knowledge?

Take a moment to think about who your business role models are by completing the "My Role Models" worksheet on the previous page.

My "bright idea"

What excites you about your business idea? If you have two or three ideas, what do you like best about each one? Where did the idea come from? How has it evolved since you started the process of turning the idea into a business?

By looking at how you initially got the inspiration for your business, you can take the next step towards determining how you might get others excited about your business also. That's the start of taking an idea and turning it into a plan, which becomes a successful business. It will also

MY "BRIGHT IDEA"

Use this space to record your initial business idea(s). This will become a starting point for defining your business concept and why it can be competitive in the marketplace, on the next page. It will also be useful as you prepare your marketing materials and write your "Elevator Pitch" in Week Six.

What is your business idea?

How did you come up with it?

What excites you about it?

MY BUSINESS CONCEPT

Answering the following questions will help you clarify your concept:

Is yours a retail, service, manufacturing, distribution, or Internet business?

What industry does it belong to?

What products or services do you sell?

What improved features/services or added value do you provide? What makes you unique or special?

Who do you see as your potential customers?

What is your overall marketing and sales strategy?

Which companies (or types of companies) do you think of as your competition?

What do you think will make customers buy from you instead of your competitors?

be useful to have a record of what initially inspired you to refer to from time-to-time, especially as your business grows. Use the worksheet on page 13 to record your initial business idea.

4. Describe your business concept

Meeting needs is the basis of all business. You can devise a wonderful new machine, but if it doesn't address some real and important need or desire, people won't buy it, and your business will fail. Even Thomas Edison recognised this fact when he said, "Anything that won't sell, I don't want to invent."

Identify needs

Now that you know what your spark and passion is about your idea, use the worksheet at left to determine how your product or service will meet new or existing needs in the marketplace.

A concept's success often hinges on whether it does something newer or better than anyone else. Being new or better can take many forms:

- **Something new.** A new product, service, feature, or technology.

- **Something better.** This could be an improvement on an existing product or service encompassing more features, lower price, greater reliability, faster speed, increased convenience, or enhanced technology.

- **An underserved or new market.** This is a market for which there is greater demand than competitors can currently satisfy, an unserved location, or a small part of an overall market—a niche market—that hasn't yet been dominated by other competitors. Sometimes, markets become underserved when large companies abandon or neglect smaller portions of their current customer base.

- **New delivery system or distribution channel.** New technologies, particularly the Internet, allow companies to reach customers more efficiently. This has opened up many new opportunities for businesses to provide products or services less expensively, to a wider geographic area, or with far greater choice.

- **Increased integration.** This occurs when a product is both manufactured and sold by the same company, or when a company offers more services or products in one location.

BASIC BUSINESS DESCRIPTION

Use this worksheet to develop a business description for your business.
For example, a finished description might read:

"AAA, Ltd., is a funky, imaginative food products and service company aimed at offering high-quality, moderately priced, occasionally unusual foods using only natural ingredients. We view ourselves as partners with our customers, our employees, our community, and our environment, and we take personal responsibility in our actions towards each. We aim to become a regionally recognised brand name, capitalising on the sustained interest in Thai food. Our goal is moderate growth, annual profitability, and maintaining our sense of humour."

Describe the following in one sentence:

Core business concept:
Core business values:
Core business goals:
Core financial goals:
Corporate culture:

Now take a stab at combining these sentences into one comprehensive statement.
You will revisit and rewrite it several times, but you'll need a succinct business description for your business plan, investors, employees, and others, so get something on paper now.

Your concept should be strong in at least one area. If not, you should ask yourself how your company will be truly competitive.

Outline specifics

Okay, so you have your inspiration, and you've seen an opportunity in the market…now how do those translate into your particular business concept? Exactly what are you going to sell? To whom? How?

The "Basic Business Description" worksheet at left helps you outline the specifics of your business as you see them at this early point. You'll be more successful if you have a clear concept of critical business aspects such as your target market, competition, industry, and so on.

Don't worry if you aren't entirely certain about the answers to your "Basic Business Description." Fill in the answers anyway. You'll use these specifics to guide the research you'll do in Week Two, and you'll continue to refine your business concept as you go along.

5. Identify your strategic position

The late Eugene Kleiner, one of the world's most successful venture capitalists, once told me that most companies don't know what business they're in. By this he meant that most businesspeople don't understand the true basis on which they compete. Yes, they know how to make their products, invent their technologies, but they don't really understand what makes their customers buy from them.

Today, defining a strategic position is as important for the proverbial corner shop small business as it is for a high technology company. It's not enough to hang out a shingle that says, "I sell shoes," or "I sell e-commerce technology." You have to have something that's unique, that few others can offer, that makes your customers want to buy from you.

You have to understand how you meaningfully differentiate yourself from the competition—your strategic position in the marketplace.

Of course, the best strategic position is just to be better than the competition—the tennis racket you've invented enables players to hit harder, the graphic designs you create are more memorable. But those things are often a matter of judgment and hard to prove.

So, how do you develop a clear distinction between yourself and the competition? Your company's strategic position can be based on:

- **Serving a specific niche in the market**
- **Unique features of your product or service**
- **Exceptional customer service**
- **Price**
- **Convenience, or**
- **Anything that significantly distinguishes you from others who offer similar services or products.**

The more you understand about your own company—and how you differ from others—the better able you are to compete.

6. Decide whether you want partners

Marks and Spencer, Hewlett and Packard, Bradford and Bingley. Great partnerships often make great companies. But just as often, bad partnerships destroy good companies.

Nothing affects your day-to-day work life more than the people you work with. Yes, work can be satisfying when you have challenging tasks, play with cool technology, or make lots money, but whether you feel like getting out of bed in the morning can greatly be influenced by who you're going to work with that day.

Partners not only affect your mood but your bottom line as well. They share, or may even control, ownership of your company. Spend time getting to know the business skills, attitudes, and aspirations of any potential partners—even if you've been friends or acquaintances for many years. Find out whether their goals, work style, and values fit yours.

If you are going to take on a partner, carefully consider why you want or need one. As you start your business, you may feel uncertain about being on your own, but that feeling of uncertainty may pass quickly. A partner will be around for a long, long time. Remember, partners own a piece of the business. Even if you bring in someone with only a minority interest as a partner, your future is tied to them.

Make certain your expectations of what you'll get out of a partnership are realistic. Are they willing to work as hard as you? Do they bring the same level of talent or skill (although perhaps in a different area) as you? Do they have the same long-term view of where they want to be?

You have more leeway, legally, to ask questions of potential partners than of employees. Of course, make certain your potential partner is honest, but also examine their personal attitudes, how they handle stress, how much money they need and how soon, family or other demands on their time, and any other issues that may affect your working relationship.

The best way to take on a partner is with clear-cut definitions of responsibilities and authority. It's nice to believe you will make every decision together, but that's not realistic. Who, in the end, gets to call the shots? And be careful about going to work with a friend—often both the business and the friendship suffers.

QUESTIONS TO ASK   POTENTIAL PARTNERS

✓ Why are you going into business?

✓ What are your personal goals for this business?

✓ How much money do you need now? How much money will you need over the next 12 months? 24 months? 36 months?

✓ How much money are you able and willing to invest in the company, if any?

✓ How big a company would you like this to be one day?

✓ How much time do you have to devote to the business?

✓ What other obligations do you have, both business and personal, that will affect your commitment of time, money and attention?

✓ How do you see decisions being made? By whom?

✓ What areas of responsibility do you feel capable of taking on?

✓ What areas of responsibility do you want to be in charge of?

✓ How formal/informal do you like to be about such things as work hours, dress code, etc.?

✓ Is your family supportive of this commitment?

✓ Have you ever been in a partnership before? What happened?

✓ What are your fears in this partnership?

DISCUSSING PARTNERSHIP TERMS

Use this worksheet to determine with your partners the terms of your partnership.
Then meet with a lawyer to draw up a formal partnership agreement.

Ownership Division. Who owns what percent?

Jobs/Responsibilities. What jobs and responsibilities does each partner have? Can partners work for any other company or do any other work on the side?

Decisions. How will general business decisions be made? What decisions does each partner have final authority on? Who has the final authority for decisions for the company as a whole?

Communication. How will you communicate on a regular basis? How will serious disputes be resolved?

Exit Strategy and Dissolution Agreement. What happens if one partner wants to leave the business or move? What if one partner wants to sell the company? What happens if a partner dies or becomes disabled?

Other:

If you're going into business with other people, even a spouse or friend, formalise your arrangement with a written partnership agreement. Take the time to work out as many details as you can. Be certain to include a way to buy each other (or the other's heirs) out of the business. A messy "divorce" from a business partner is as difficult as a messy marital divorce—with potentially greater financial consequences. Drawing up an agreement now will help avoid difficulties if you later decide to go your separate ways.

Use the guide "Questions to Ask: Potential Partners" on page 19 to discuss the nature of your relationship. The worksheet "Discussing Partnership Terms" at left outlines important issues that can later become part of a formal agreement, drawn up with the help of a lawyer.

7. Decide whether you want investors

You may have heard that it's best to start a business using OPM—"Other People's Money," but don't just rush out looking for investors. Choosing to get an investor is a big decision.

You are almost always tied to your investors for the life of your business. Remember, there usually isn't any easy way out of a relationship with an investor; in fact, if you have to come to a parting of the ways, your investors may have more ability to get rid of you than you will have to get rid of them. So proceed carefully!

Don't forget—investors legally own a piece of your business, and they have certain rights under the law. They are entitled not only to a share of your profits but have other rights as well. They are also entitled to a share of your losses for tax purposes. The involvement of investors makes dealing with legal issues, decision-making, taxes, and many other issues more complicated and expensive. And if things go wrong, having investors can make everything a lot messier.

If you decide you absolutely need investors, make certain you spend as much time as possible getting to know any potential investor—after all, you're tied to each other for a long time. It's unlikely you can ask as many probing questions of a potential investor as you can a potential partner because investors usually view the investment process as an examination of you—not the other way round. Nevertheless, find out if they've invested in other companies before. If so, speak to other entrepreneurs who've worked with them. What are their financial and busi-

RED TAPE ALERT! Even if you never use the word "partner," if you and a friend decide to start selling used golf balls on the Internet together, in the eyes of the law, you've become partners. The best way for things to stay friendly between partners is to have a clearly defined partnership agreement before you begin the company. Prepare a legally-binding contract spelling out the terms of your partnership: who owns what percent, how decisions are made, what happens to the company if one or more of the partners wishes to leave, how and whether additional partners can be added, etc. It is also advisable to work out a "Buy/Sell" agreement, so the terms of how and to whom a partner can leave or sell their interest in the business are clear. You may want provisions limiting their ability to sell their interest to others and, in the case of a partner's death or disability, to have other partners buy out their heirs at a fair price—you don't necessarily want to be running the business with your partners' spouse or child.

ness motivations for investing? Are those goals a good fit with your own? How much control do they want in the business?

Of course, when you need money to start a business, you may feel lucky to get the money you need from anyone. But over time, if you have a fearful, intrusive, or controlling investor, you may soon regret being involved with them.

If you decide you need investors, you'll find more information in Week Five, including Questions to Ask before you accept financing (page 227) and a worksheet with an Investor Comparison Chart (page 224).

8. Consider potential exit strategies

When you're building a business, you don't spend a lot of time envisioning how you'll eventually get out of it. Oh, maybe you think one day you'll make enough money to retire, but while you can envision yourself golfing or gardening, what's happened to your company? You need an "exit plan."

An exit plan is a long-term strategy for transferring ownership of your company to others. The idea of thinking of an exit when you're just starting out may seem incongruous. After all, you hardly know what you're going to be doing next month; why try to figure out what you're going to do with your company ten or twenty years from now?

If you're looking for an investor in your company, they'll want to know your long-term goals and will ask you to spell out an exit strategy. They want to know how they're going to get their money back.

If you're going to have a partner, then discussing your exit strategy reduces the friction that comes when you have unspoken but differing exit assumptions. You may hope to grow the business substantially and later sell, while they may want to maintain the business at a modest level and perhaps someday have a relative take over.

Even if you own the company yourself and hope to have it last through the ages, an exit plan helps direct the growth of your company. If, for instance, you would ideally like to be acquired by a larger company, you might target your product development and marketing efforts in ways that would interest acquiring companies.

There are a number of ways you can exit your company or have the value of the company become liquid:

- **Sell.** This is often the simplest way to get value out. All types of companies can be sold, not just retail or manufacturing enterprises. Professional practices are "bought into" by new partners, or a one-person consulting business can be sold to someone who wants a built-in customer base.

- **Be acquired.** Your company may be a good fit for a larger company that wants the part of the market, capabilities, or technologies you have developed.

- **Merge.** This is similar to being acquired but the assets of the merging companies form a new entity.

- **"Go public."** When you issue shares in your company that are traded in a stock market—an initial public offering (IPO)—it is referred to as "going public." This doesn't necessarily mean you depart from management of the company, but you now have a way to get money for your ownership interest by selling some of your personal shares.

- **Have family members take over.** When Levi Strauss started selling blue jeans, he probably didn't envision a family-owned company bearing his name 150 years later. Even if you know you'd like this to happen, you need a plan. Your family members might not want to or be capable of running the company.

■ **Employee buy-out.** An excellent way to keep your company together and to retain the jobs you've created is to structure a way for either key management or employees as a whole to buy the company. A share ownership scheme can help them finance the purchase and give you the cash you need.

■ **Go out of business.** This is the easiest exit (assuming you have no debts or major employee commitments), but you also get the least financial reward. Sometimes though, you just want to close up shop and get on with the rest of your life.

9. Discuss the impact of starting a business with your family

When you start a business, it has an impact on everyone around you, especially your family. You'll almost certainly have to make financial sacrifices, have less free time for them, and have more things on your mind than before you started. If you're married, owning a business may have legal and/or tax implications for your spouse.

Sit down and fully discuss your plans with the other people in your life who may be directly affected. Help them to understand what you see as the opportunities, as well as being clear about the potential risks and probable sacrifices.

Ask for their input, too. They may have suggestions of ways they can be supportive. In most small businesses, family members frequently lend a hand. Allow them to share some of their fears or concerns so you get a realistic idea of what's on their minds. Discuss ways to make certain that your family responsibilities are met even while you build your business. Make them feel a part of your new, exciting adventure.

Be careful, however, about asking for loans or investments from family or close friends—you may risk both the business and the personal relationship. Of course, there are exceptions: if the person understands the nature of your business, truly appreciates the risks, and is someone with whom you can communicate well, the situation may work. *Always* have loan or investment papers drawn up with the terms of the repayment or investment absolutely clear.

More information about getting and working with investors can be found in Week Five.

10. Get some advice

One of the best, least-known services provided by the government to small businesses is a national network of Business Links. These provide free one-on-one counselling and low-cost training programmes to small businesses and start-up entrepreneurs. Business Link Advisors are trained professionals; most have run small businesses themselves as well as having expertise in particular aspects of management.

The structure of each Business Link varies depending on location and who is running it. Many will have books and materials to assist you in planning and running your business. Don't forget your bank will also have information and advice on this.

Business Links offer a variety of services including training sessions and one to one advice. To find your local BL go to www.businesslink.gov.uk and type your post code into the box – and while you're there have a look at the excellent advice on structuring your business and fitting into legislation that's offered on the site itself.

Business Links offer assistance with many of the following:

- **Understanding business laws and regulations**
- **Sources of market and competitive research**
- **Business plan development guidance**
- **Computer software training programmes**
- **Budgeting**

Years ago, I turned to a Business Link for assistance in doing a trade-mark search (this was before the Internet made it easy to do a first level search). The Business Link staff was helpful, supportive, and encouraging. Business Link Advisors can assist you not only in starting your business, but as you grow your business as well.

I highly recommend checking out your local Business Link sooner rather than later. You can find a link to a list of Business Links on the Internet or check your local Yellow Pages listings. Set up an appointment with a counsellor to discuss your business, doing business research, and for ongoing guidance as your business grows.

ACCOMPLISHMENT #2:
Create your company identity

Tasks:

☐ 1. Choose a name

☐ 2. Check out trademarks

☐ 3. Secure a domain name

☐ 4. Consider logos, straplines, and colours

☐ 5. Get a graphic designer

Right from Week One, you're going to be eager to begin working on one of the most challenging and creative aspects of starting your own business—developing your company identity: name, image, logo, strapline, and so on.

Coming up with a company identity can be fun, creative, and exciting. But if you're not careful, it can also paralyze you. You may think that finding just the *right* name or logo is absolutely critical for success.

Please, don't let this process overwhelm you. While choosing the right name and image for your company *is* important, it doesn't determine your company's future. After all, not many people would consider names such as "Microsoft," "Sainsbury's," or the "Walt Disney Company" as being particularly inspired or critical to the company's eventual success.

Nevertheless, creating your company identity certainly is an important part of getting your business underway. Your corporate identity helps customers remember you, understand what you do, and even develop a certain feeling about you. Your company name and logo make your business feel "real," both to you and to potential customers, suppliers, and others. Your identity is your brand image.

The key elements to a corporate identity are:

- **Name**
- **Logo**
- **Strapline**
- **Colours**

In addition, you might have other unique, distinguishing elements that make up your identity, such as clever or unusual packaging.

Once you've developed a certain identity, you'll use those elements consistently and repeatedly—on your business cards, stationery, signs, advertising, vehicles, uniforms, and website.

Creating an identity can be done very inexpensively or cost thousands of pounds. You may want to use the services of a graphic designer to help you create your logo and other aspects of your company's image.

1. Choose a name

I collect cute business names: "All You Knead," (a bakery), "The Barking Lot" (a dog groomer), "Shear Ecstasy" (a hair salon). A clever business name can be an excellent marketing tool—helping make your company memorable—but coming up with a good name can seem frustrating. Big companies spend thousands of pounds researching names, and sometimes even they fail.

In small companies, *you* are the brand, and usually the best name for your company is your own, perhaps adding a descriptive phrase to clarify what you do. My first business was called "Abrams Business Strategies" since I developed business and marketing plans.

If you plan on growing your business substantially though, you may not want to use your own name, or any person's name. Having a name that is closely associated with the owner may later make a company harder to sell and can create expectations among customers that they will be getting personal attention from the owner.

BUSINESS NAME COMPARISON CHART

Questions	Name	Name
What are the business names you have considered so far?		
What about the name tells your customers what you do?		
What about the name tells your customers what they get?		
What about the name conveys a feeling? What kind of feeling?		
Are the names already trademarked by another business?		
Are there companies with similar or confusing names?		
Was the name trademarked in a different category? Which one? By whom?		
Who likes the name? Why?		
Who dislikes the name? Why?		
What available domain name (i.e. web address) would work well with the name?		
Other comments / questions about each name:		

BUSINESS NAME COMPARISON CHART

Name	Name	Name

A good company name achieves several goals:

- **Communicates the correct information.** You want to avoid anything in your business name that could substantially confuse potential customers about what you do. So even if you think your name is crystal clear (e.g., Jim's Photo Services), ask a few other people if they can easily figure out what business you're in (e.g., do they think you're a photographer, a film processor, provide digital photo touch-ups?) A very clear company name, such as "Main Street Volvo Repair," immediately lets customers know what to expect, but watch out if your services later change or if you run into trademark problems—see below.

- **Conveys the right feeling.** You generally want to choose a name with positive connotations: a day spa named "Haven" or "Oasis" transmits the sense that customers are going to escape the stresses in their lives. Even words such as "Main Street," or another location tells potential customers that the service is local and convenient.

- **Won't get dated quickly.** Be careful not to choose names too closely identified with recent trends or that are too limiting. You are likely to change the scope of your products or services over time. Look at all those e-commerce companies that had to drop the words "dot com" from their company names. When Twentieth Century Fox Film Studios was founded in 1935 (merging Fox and Twentieth Century studios), the name "Twentieth Century" seemed associated with the idea of something young and new. Of course, by the end of that century, it no longer seemed fresh, and the company now uses just the name "Fox" for some of its entertainment units.

- **Is easy to spell.** If a name is too hard to spell, it becomes harder for a potential customer to remember. Spelling becomes even more important when you use your company's name as part of your website domain name or if you're in a business where clients have to spell your company's name often.

- **Is easy to pronounce.** People have a harder time remembering names they can't say easily, and they feel uncomfortable doing business with companies whose names they can't pronounce. That's why on the back of their chocolate bar wrappers, Ghirardelli prints a pronunciation guide.

- **Is memorable.** Obviously, if clients or customers have an easier time remembering your name, they're more likely to do business with you again. This isn't absolutely necessary or always even possible. In fact, a company with a straight-forward name, such as "Milton Keynes Chiropractic Clinic," may develop a better business than a company with a cute name.

In the end, however, one of the most important considerations is whether *you* like the name and feel comfortable with it. After all, you're the one who's going to be seeing it and saying it the most.

Most importantly, don't get stuck trying to decide on your name, slowing down the start of your business. At some point, you just need to make a choice and get on with it.

Use the worksheet on pages 28–29 to compare some of the names you're thinking of for your business, and their pros and cons.

2. Check out trademarks

You're thrilled! You've settled on a name for your new breakfast cereal company: "Yummy Tummy." You've even invented a cartoon character, "Yummy Tummy Tillie," to symbolise your brand. You're ready to set the world on fire!

Not so fast. Before you can make your company a household name, you need to make sure you can use and protect that name. You don't want to invest money and time building "brand equity"—value associated with the name of your company—just to discover someone else is already using "Yummy Tummy."

That's where trademark laws come in.

When you acquire the rights to a trademark, you get legal protection from other companies using your company's name, logos, straplines, or other distinctive marks on competing products or services.

Even when you are granted a trademark, you don't "own" the name in all instances. As part of the trademark application process, you'll indicate the specific category or categories of products or services for which you'll be using the name. For instance, if you're using "Yummy Tummy"

ABOUT TRADEMARKS

What is a trademark?

- A **trademark** is a word, phrase, symbol or design, or a combination of words, phrases, symbols or designs, that identifies and distinguishes the source of the goods of one party from those of others.

Is registration of my mark required?

No. You can establish rights in a mark based on legitimate use of the mark. However, registration provides several advantages, e.g.,

- Constructive notice to the public of the registrant's claim of ownership of the mark;

- A legal presumption of the registrant's ownership of the mark and the registrant's exclusive right to use the mark nationwide on or in connection with the goods and/or services listed in the registration;

- The ability to bring an action concerning the mark in federal court; and

- The use of the UK registration as a basis to obtain registration in foreign countries

for breakfast cereal, someone else could get the rights to use the same name for unrelated products or services—a weight-loss programme, for instance.

There are, of course, limits to what you can trademark. Indeed, it's often frustrating to find that you can't trademark the simplest names. That's because the UK Intellectual Property Office requires a mark to be "distinctive" and not simply "descriptive." For instance, you can't get a trademark for a health resort called "Spa," because it's merely descriptive. But you almost certainly could trademark the name "Spa" for a brand of body lotions (assuming it wasn't already trademarked by someone else).

In fact, if you're inventing a whole new product category, you may need to come up with a generic way to describe the category in order to trademark your chosen name. A client of mine, Patrick McConnell, invented a dry-land snowboard, which he called the MountainBoard. To get that name trademarked, however, Patrick had to come up with a generic term—"all terrain board"—to avoid his brand name being viewed as merely descriptive.

Doing a trademark search

Getting the trademark process underway is fairly simple, but you'll want to discuss the trademark process when you see an attorney (Week Three), as well as discussing other protections of your "intellectual property"— such as copyrights and patents.

To get started on your name and trademark search, begin at the website of the UK Intellectual Property Office. Find the section for Trademarks and follow the links for "Search."

Try different ways to search ("New User Form," "Structured Form," etc.) to see the various results. Begin by searching as broadly as possible—singular and plural forms of your words, similar words, alternate spellings, and so on. Results may show both "live" and "dead" marks. Dead marks are those that have lapsed by previous owners.

Keep in mind that even if a particular name or mark does not show up as being taken, it does not necessarily mean you will be able to trademark the name/mark. Some names may already be in use in interstate commerce but may not have been officially registered. Other names/marks may not be allowed to be registered as trademarks. So don't print up millions of pounds worth of brochures just yet!

And remember, you may run into difficulty if you use a name that is similar to a bigger, better-known company even if you think you can get a trademark. McDonald's, for instance, has been very effective in keeping others from using the "Mc" as a prefix for many different kinds of products and companies. A juice bar company was able to keep other juice bars from using names starting with the letter "J" just by taking them to court. Often, it's the company with the biggest bank account and most lawyers, rather than the ones with the law on their side, that control a name or trademark.

If you are going to spend a great deal of money investing in a name and trademark, you might consider using a professional trademark search firm or hiring a trademark lawyer to conduct a more complete search.

3. Secure a domain name

An important part of choosing a business name and getting a trademark is researching the availability of an appropriate website address. Before the Internet, for instance, you might have happily been able to do business in one state without ever being confused with a business using the same name in another state. Now, one of you puts up a site on the Internet, and customers might not know who's who.

A "domain name" is the name by which an Internet site is identified and found. It is often referred to, somewhat incorrectly, as your company's "URL" or universal resource locator.

Hot Link

Register your website domain name at Network Solutions. **www.networksolutions. com**

To find out whether others may be using the name you have selected— or similar names—go to the "whois" section of the Network Solutions website (Network Solutions is the official keeper of the domain name registry). Type in the name you'd like to use along with the suffix. For example, to see if the name of the company publishing this book is being used, you'd type in the words: planningshop.com.

Many of the most obvious and popular domain names are likely to already be taken. Even if you are able to get a trademark, someone else may legally have the rights to that domain name, especially since many companies can have the same trademark name in different categories.

Try to find a domain name that is:

- **identical or similar to your company name**
- **related to the product or service you sell**

- **easy to spell**
- **easy to remember**
- **not likely to be confused with another domain name**

Don't worry if you can't find just the right domain name. You'll find that even big companies have somewhat awkward domain names because they weren't able to secure their own name.

Remember, a domain name is only as good as the marketing budget—and the business—to which it's attached. The success of your business does not rise or fall on your domain name—no matter how cute, memorable, or descriptive. Most potential customers learn of you through means other than your website: business cards, brochures, networking events, advertising, word-of-mouth, etc. If they like you and your company, they'll be willing to type in "www.hardtorememberurl.com."

4. Consider logos, straplines, and colours

Your company identity consists of more than just your company name. The colours you choose, the typeface you use, and what kind of strapline and logo you develop (if any) convey a message to potential customers. Right from the beginning of your business, you should consider what message you want to send and select a corporate identity appropriate for the type of business you're starting. You should then use those elements of your corporate identity consistently throughout all your marketing and communication materials.

Logos

All of us are familiar with logos: the Nike "swoosh," McDonald's golden arches, Apple Computer's apple-with-a-bite. A logo is an image associated with your company, giving the public another way to remember you.

Visual images make your company more memorable. There's a reason for this: people learn things and remember things in many different ways. When prospective customers see your logo as well as see or hear your company's name, they're using more of their brains to process the information—both verbal and visual. So you make more of a mental impact when people associate you with both words and images.

A good logo conveys something positive about your company. If you don't have the money to have a logo designed, an inexpensive way to add a visual element to your business name is to just add geometric elements: lines, squares, diamonds, and so on. In my first business—business consulting—I used three sideways triangles, suggesting to prospective clients that I would help them move their business forward:

A logo doesn't have to be a drawing or illustration—you can make an "illustration" of just words. This is called a "logotype," and it can be very effective. Think of Coca-Cola:

When we were developing a logo for The Planning Shop, we wanted an image that would convey the message that products from The Planning Shop enable people to "complete" their business planning projects. We decided that the concept of the last piece of a puzzle—fitting into a written document (a business plan, for instance)—would visually convey that feeling of completion. Here's what we came up with:

Use the "Creating My Identity" worksheet on page 38 to make notes or drawings of possible logos for your business.

Straplines

Many companies use a motto or strapline either to better explain the nature of the business or to create a feeling about the company or product.

A strapline helps customers remember what is unique about your business:

- **"Personalised service at practical prices"**
- **"Legal services for the real estate industry"**

Straplines don't have to be "catchy" to be memorable to your target audience. "Manufacturers of packing materials for technology products" may seem boring but be very effective if you make and sell boxes for computers. This lets your potential customers know—and reminds current customers—you specialise in exactly what they need.

Straplines can become the basis of your advertising and marketing pieces. Of course, you would use your strapline in all your advertising. But even if you don't have much of a marketing budget, you can use your strapline on your business cards, packaging, stationery, even the end of emails.

You don't have to have a strapline, and you certainly don't have to choose one before you even open your doors. But developing a strapline helps you clarify what makes your business special and enables you to sum up your competitive position in just a few words.

Colours

Many people start their businesses without giving colours much thought, and yet most of us intend to use some colours in our business—in our décor, on our business cards, brochures, packaging, website, and so on. What often happens is that you end up using one colour for one thing (let's say a brochure), another colour for something else (for your stationery, perhaps) and yet another colour elsewhere (maybe your website).

The result? You're losing the opportunity to develop a strong brand image for your company and perhaps even confusing your customer.

Instead, coming up with a consistent use of colour—your "colour palette"—gives you another tool to help customers remember who you are and for you to convey a feeling about your company.

Some colours are associated with certain feelings. Blue is considered calming and reassuring so banks and financial institutions often use blue. While red is considered lucky for some ethnic groups, it's viewed as a sign of danger or action to others, so consider who your target market is. Other colours have developed other associations: pink is viewed as femi-

Hot Link
The Colour Marketing Group forecasts colour trends for the next 12–18 months for a variety of industries. **www. colourmarketing.org**

CREATING MY IDENTITY

Use the space below to begin developing your corporate identity. You may want to draw pictures, as well as use words and phrases, to develop the look, feel, and message you want to convey.
You will continue this process in Week Six.

Business name

Strapline and keywords for marketing material

Logo

Colours

Distinct product design

Distinct packaging

Decor, employee clothing, or other unique identifying features

nine, pastels are associated with babies. Colours also go through fads, so be careful to choose a colour that won't be dated too quickly.

Since referring to colours just by generic names ("blue," "teal blue," etc.) is very imprecise, professionals use a system to identify particular colours. You'll want to learn the "PMS" numbers (which stands for "Pantone Matching System") of the specific colour(s) you choose so you can give future printers and designers the exact colours you want.

Since you're likely to be using your colour palette on your website, keep in mind that some colours do not display well on computer monitors. Check your colours on several different monitors before finalising your choice.

Be careful also about how many colours you use in your business. If you use too many, it can become expensive to print your stationery, business cards, packaging, and so on.

Write down your thoughts for logos, straplines, colours and other aspects of your corporate identity on the "Creating My Identity" worksheet at left.

5. Meet with a graphic designer

If you can afford it, you may want a graphic designer to help you create your corporate identity: logos, website, stationery, etc. Obviously, when you hire a graphic designer, you should look at their portfolio (samples of previous work for other clients) to see if you like their style and feel they have the right background for you. But once you've committed yourself to working with a designer, the next step is to help them understand your vision.

Have the designer read the business concept and description statements you developed on pages 14 and 16. Give the designer a sense of your goals and values, so they can consider them in the design. Show them other visual images you like so they can get a sense of your tastes and preferences.

Use the guide "Questions to Ask: Graphic Designers" (next page) as a starting point. The more information you give your designer to work with, the better they can develop a corporate identity that works for you.

| QUESTIONS TO ASK | GRAPHIC DESIGNERS |

✓ **Ask about:**   Their experience.

How they handle the design process.

Who's going to do the work? The person you meet, assistants, or others?

What fees/costs are involved? What deliverables will you receive?

✓ **Ask for:**   At least three to five design options included in the initial fee.

Both black-and-white and colour digital versions of your identity system.

Digital templates for all aspects of your identity system you select: business cards, stationery, fax cover sheets, etc.

Colour palette and numbers, both for print and for the Internet.

A signed agreement giving you ownership and copyright of all designs (very important!).

✓ **Tell them:**   What the company name represents and what your company does.

Who your target market is: their ages, industries, and concerns.

What you want your customers to feel about you.

Whether you want a traditional or more innovative approach.

What colour palettes you like or dislike.

Who your competitors are and how you're different.

ACCOMPLISHMENT #3:
Get organised

Tasks:

☐ 1. Set up physical files

☐ 2. Set up computer files

☐ 3. Set up a contact management system

☐ 4. Keep track of your company's "vital statistics"

☐ 5. Keep track of expenses

Starting any new, big project can seem overwhelming. There's so much to do, so many things to think about. Some of the challenges are fun: coming up with a name for your business, creating new products, thinking up innovative marketing ideas. Some of the tasks don't seem such fun: setting up a budget, going to a lawyer, getting business licenses.

With so many things to do, it's easy to forget or overlook some of the most important things. So right from Week One, start keeping track of all the basics and get organised so you don't lose critical information you'll need later.

1. Set up physical files

Trust me: you're about to get a lot of stuff. You're quickly going to accumulate a whole lot of tangible stuff (reports, brochures, samples, contracts) as well as intangible stuff (information, data, advice, prices, etc.) You'll be gathering information on customers, competitors, suppliers, distributors. You'll be researching and evaluating computers, facilities, and vendors. You'll be given names and numbers of people who can help you. And you'll be spending money—money you can later deduct as business expenses *if* you keep track of it and keep receipts.

All this stuff can overwhelm you. Instead of feeling like you're making progress, you'll feel completely over your head. And if you don't stay on top of your stuff, it can directly affect your chance of success—and your bottom line!

FILE FOLDER LABELS

Cut out these labels and fold them in half. Then, insert them into plastic tabs for hanging file folders.

Accountant	Distributors	Loans
Accounts Payable	Entertainment/Meals	Market Research
Accounts Receivable	Equipment	Mileage/Parking
Advertising	Insurance	Names/Trademarks
Bank Accounts	Investors	Payroll
Customer Contracts	Lawyer	Suppliers
Employee Contracts	Lease	Tax Matters
Customer Leads	Licenses	Travel

So, set up both physical files—to hold all that tangible stuff, including receipts—and digital files on your computer to hold all that intangible stuff: your notes, contact info, price comparisons, and so on.

Get in the habit—right from Week One—of putting the stuff you gather (tangible or intangible) in the appropriate file as you go along. If you wait until later ("I'll put this stuff away this weekend"), those piles of paper will just get larger and larger and larger…

In addition, I'd recommend getting a good size box (like a large plastic storage tub) to keep all your bulkier items (such as samples, large brochures, research studies) in one place and easily retrievable.

At left you'll find file folder labels you can cut out or copy and use to set up your physical filing system.

2. Set up computer files

In addition to all the physical stuff you're going to accumulate, you're going to pile up information even faster.

While you can start by keeping track of information in a notebook, pretty soon you're going to find it hard to retrieve information you desperately need.

Also, it's likely that you're going to be doing a lot of research on the Internet—regarding competitors, pricing, sources, and so on—and you'll find it much easier to keep track of this data if you've got a system set up right on your computer.

So start setting up computer files as you gather information. You can use the headings on the file folder labels at left as a guide for setting up files and folders on your computer.

Another good habit to get into, right from the start, is to make note of the sources and date of any information you find. This is particularly important for data such as pricing, market data, sources, and vendors.

3. Set up a contact management system

People who do not seem particularly important during the early stages of your business may be very useful at a later date. It's a horrible feeling to realise a few months down the road that you met the perfect supplier or distributor, or the person who could introduce you to the right investor, but you've lost the little slip of paper with their name, phone number, and email address.

Moreover, you'll want to start building your database of potential customers, referral sources, and friends so you can later invite them to your "Grand Opening" (Week Six). Believe me, when it comes time to start your marketing programme, you'll be glad you have an easy way to identify and contact people you want to communicate with.

So, right from Week One, establish a system for retaining and retrieving individual's contact information. The best way to do this is with a "contact management" or "customer relationship management" (CRM) software program.

Contact management is so important that big corporations spend hundreds of thousands—even millions—of pounds on huge, powerful CRM systems. You don't have to. You can get by with a much simpler contact management program.

A contact management program can be as simple as an electronic "address book" such as one included as part of an email program, like Microsoft Outlook or Eudora. As a start, that's a good way to make sure you don't lose important contact information.

However, you're probably going to quickly outgrow the contact capabilities included in email programs and will want to get a dedicated contact management software program.

If yours is a sales-heavy business, you may want to invest in a sales-oriented customer management program such as ACT or Gold Mine. Intuit, the makers of Quicken and QuickBooks, also has an excellent, less expensive program: QuickBooks Customer Manager.

At the very least, set up a file on your computer for contact information. Don't just let business cards stack up.

4. Keep track of your company's vital statistics

Throughout the life of your business, there's certain information you're going to be asked over and over again, such as your Tax ID number and your date of incorporation. You'll save a lot of time and aggravation later if you start recording all important dates, numbers, and data relating to your company right from the start.

Get in the habit of writing down—in one place—all of your company's "vital statistics." Otherwise, you'll find it's annoying to have to dig through files to find the same information repeatedly.

You'll find a worksheet to keep track of all the vital statistics about your business in Week Three on page 95.

5. Keep track of expenses

In Week Five, you're going to be dealing with money matters, but don't wait until then to start keeping track of the money you spend. After all, many of your expenses may be tax deductible, and you'll want to save every penny you can when you're first opening up shop.

You can choose to wait until Week Five to ask your accountant for a recommendation of a bookkeeping software program, but at the very least, start keeping track of each and every expenditure you make right now.

week 2

GET THE INFO YOU NEED

Main accomplishments:

- ✓ Learn more about your industry
- ✓ Research your target market
- ✓ Check out your competition and find suppliers
- ✓ Consider strategic partners
- ✓ Broaden/establish your network

Make appointments with:

- ✓ Attend a community, entrepreneur, or industry organisation meeting

get the info

you need

THIS WEEK YOU'RE GOING TO SHARPEN YOUR SKILLS at finding critical business information—whether it be about your industry, target market, competitors or other business information you'll need.

Don't be put off by the word "research." It probably conjures up the image of term papers and school projects; this kind of research isn't like that. Instead, this week, you'll get shortcuts to finding reliable information to help you build your business and make decisions.

The emphasis is on finding such information fast, easily, and hopefully free (or at least pretty damned cheap).

Start with the "Learn more about your industry" section because many of the skills and sources you'll use for other types of research (for instance, your target market or suppliers) will be the same as for doing industry research.

To begin, get out your computer; most of the information-gathering will occur online. And get ready to find the information you need to build your company!

ACCOMPLISHMENT #1:

Learn more about your industry

Tasks:

☐ 1. Make a list of your research questions

☐ 2. Contact your industry association(s)

☐ 3. Do online research

1. Make a list of your research questions

Once you start looking for information, you're likely going to find more information than you need—or not find the right information at all. A good way to speed up the process of finding information is to start by making a general statement that defines the basis of your business.

For example, if you are planning to start an Internet company providing online psychological therapy, your general statement might be: "There is a profitable way to provide psychological counselling via the Internet." Next, make a list of questions that logically follow from and challenge that statement. Here are some questions you might ask about the online therapy business:

- **What companies are already providing such a service?**
- **What is the market size for all kinds of psychological counselling?**
- **What indications are there that consumers would be willing to get counselling on the Internet?**
- **What portion of the existing psychological counselling market is it reasonable to expect would transfer to online counselling?**
- **How many consumers who do not currently get counselling could you reasonably expect to be attracted to online counselling?**
- **What other companies are currently providing such online counselling services? How many are there? How many clients do they have? What is their ability to keep out new competitors? What do they charge?**
- **What are the costs involved in conducting an online therapy business?**
- **What are the key technology issues necessary to conduct such counselling, securely, on the Internet?**
- **What laws or regulations would affect the offering of such services?**

Begin your list with the "My Research Questions" worksheet on page 52. Ask yourself tough questions—it's much better to uncover unpleasant truths now rather than after you've invested your time and money.

After drawing up your list of questions, start looking for answers. Organise your market research data in the files you set up last week. Refer to it frequently as you design your marketing plan, look for funding, and launch your operation.

As you prepare your questions, jot down any ideas about where you might find answers on the worksheet "Research Sources" on page 55.

2. Contact your industry association(s)

When looking for information for your new business, the very first place to start is with an association serving your industry or related industries. No matter what industry, trade, or profession you're in, there's almost certainly at least one association covering yours. Why? Because there are over thirty thousand industry and professional associations!

You'll find industry, trade, or professional associations to be a highly valuable source of information. Most associations conduct research or collect data on trends of their industry. They monitor market size and demographics, costs, regulation, and a variety of other issues specific to their industry.

Typically, suppliers to an industry also often participate in that industry's associations. They'll exhibit at trade shows and be listed on the association's website or other directories. That makes your industry association an easy place to locate suppliers.

Most importantly, associations exist to help promote, train, and certify people in that industry. They'll hold trade shows, seminars, conventions, provide coursework, and offer joint marketing opportunities.

Let's say, for instance, you're thinking about starting a dog grooming business. You're going to want information about suppliers, costs, training, certification, marketing and as much other information as you can get your paws on. A number of organisations exist to help pet groomers.

To find a trade or industry association, you'll want to start with an online search.

MY RESEARCH QUESTIONS

For each of the following categories, list questions affecting the future of your business.
Use these questions to guide your research efforts.

Industry

What industry is my business considered part of?
What are the trade associations serving that industry?
What does the data show about the financial performance of that industry in recent years?
What does the data, and other information, show about trends in that industry?
Other:

Target Market

What geographic area do I plan on serving?
What is the demographic profile of the customers I'm planning on serving? (e.g., age, gender, income, education level)
How many people fit that target demographic profile in my target geographic area?
What are the trends affecting my target market?
Is there any data indicating buying habits or preferences of my target market?
Other:

Competition

Who are the leading competitors in terms of market share or in my geographic area?
What do my competitors charge?
What are their strengths? Shortcomings?
What are the primary methods my competitors use to attract customers?
What have been the causes of previous competitors closing (if any)?
Other:

Suppliers/Vendors

What kind of equipment, materials, and services will I need?
Who are leading and/or recommended vendors providing those?
What are the costs involved?
Other:

Other

Are there laws or regulations (e.g., environmental, planning, etc.) that typically affect my type of business?
Are there any companies that would make potential strategic partners?
Other:

Three good ways to find an industry association on the Internet are:

1. **A general online search engine,** e.g., Google. Type in the keywords associated with your industry.

Hot Link
Check out Yahoo!'s multinational list of trade associations.
dir.yahoo. com/Business_ and_Economy/ Organizations/Trade_ Associations/

2. **An online directory,** e.g., Yahoo!. Look in subdirectories for "Business and Economy," or Business-to-Business, or Business Directories. Check "Professional Organisations" as well as "Trade" or "Industry" Associations.

3. **"The Trade Associations Forum"** (www.taforum.org) sees itself as a place for promoting the very best in trading practices and there is a lot of sound business advice on the site. The most useful element to the start-up business is the searchable directory which is easy to find. It's worth mentioning that websites change and are updated often, so if when you read this book the taforum.org website has moved or changed you can always try searching Google for trade associations and your chosen trade.

The difficulty is that trade associations often use names that aren't always obvious. For instance, if you typed in the word "dog groomer," you might not find what you wanted. So check other words, such as "pet groomer" or "veterinary."

When you search for associations, you may find you come up with a dozen or more, so start with groups that contain the name "National," "International," or "British," rather than local organisations. Don't be afraid to look at national trade organisations that aren't from your country as they often have information such as standards, glossaries, other site listings, etc.

3. Do online research

In addition to your industry association, you'll find a substantial amount of industry information and data on the Internet. Of course, you'll want to make certain the information is accurate and up-to-date. Be careful to rely on information from trustworthy sources, such as recognised market research companies. If possible, when using data from media sources (such as newspapers and magazines), find the original source of the data; journalists, after all, have limited space and have to edit information,

RESEARCH SOURCES

Type of information	Source	Website
UK Government	National archives (including census information)	www.nationalarchives.gov.uk
	National statistics	www.statistics.gov.uk
	Business Link, including Government documents and forms	www.businesslink.gov.uk
Local/regional information	Each council has a website	Usually www.nameofcouncil.gov.uk
Company information	Companies House	www.companieshouse.gov.uk
	Dun&Bradstreet	www.dnb.co.uk
Trade associations	Trade Associations Forum	www.tagforum.org

often leaving out data that might be important for your planning.

The key to finding industry-specific information is to be patient and diligent. You'll have to go to many sites and look around. When you find a site of interest—let's say an industry association site—follow links from that site (look for hypertext links saying things like "Related Links").

Another key is to visit websites of industries or associations you plan to market to. For instance, as a dog groomer, you might look for any local dog-owner websites or local pet shop websites. They may give you ideas for marketing opportunities as well as help you learn more about your local market. Sometimes, you can buy membership lists, giving you a built-in database of sales leads.

Look for established market research companies in your field. In technology, for instance, some of the major market research companies are Forrester and Dataquest. To find market research in your industry, do a search in a search engine by using the name of the industry plus terms like "market research."

Hot Link

Use Google's special news search engine to look for recent news about your industry. **news.google.com**

Don't forget to check for news stories about topics related to your industry. You can look at general and specific media sites and use their search and archive capabilities.

You'll find lots of information online, but I'm also a big believer in the real world. Follow your online information hunt with real-world activities, particularly attending trade shows. Get out there and talk to people, including suppliers, potential customers, even competitors. Who knows? Perhaps other dog groomers will give you a leg up on your research, and you'll find that business isn't such a dog-eat-dog world after all.

ACCOMPLISHMENT #2:
Research your target market

Tasks:

☐ **1. Define your target market**

☐ **2. Determine if there are enough customers**

WHO ARE MY CUSTOMERS?

Describe who your customers are in each of the following categories. You'll find that the number of customers in each category grows the closer you get to the "end user."

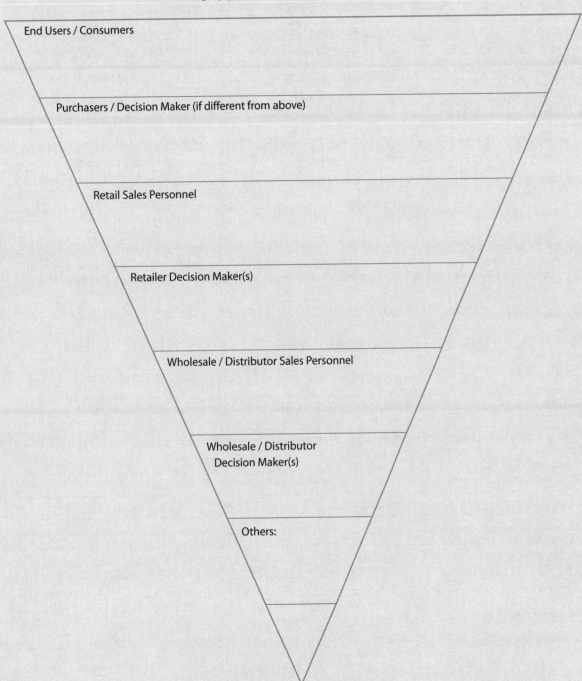

End Users / Consumers

Purchasers / Decision Maker (if different from above)

Retail Sales Personnel

Retailer Decision Maker(s)

Wholesale / Distributor Sales Personnel

Wholesale / Distributor Decision Maker(s)

Others:

MY CUSTOMER PROFILE

Rank the characteristics of your customers that are most important in determining how receptive they'll be to your product or service. For the characteristics that have no bearing on whether or not they'll buy from you, leave the space blank.

_____ Gender	_____ Education level	_____ Children in household
_____ Age	_____ Race or Ethnicity	_____ Home ownership
_____ Income level	_____ Religious affiliation	_____ Recreational activities
_____ Occupation	_____ Marital status	_____ Proximity to your business

Rank the characteristics of your product or service that are most important to your target customers.

_____ Price	_____ Convenience	_____ Product Features
_____ Service	_____ Reliability	_____ Design
_____ Status	_____ Other:_____	_____ Other:_____

Now describe your customers according to the characteristics you have identified. Start with the characteristic you ranked as most important, providing details on how you think that characteristic will influence your customers' buying decisions. You may need to continue this process on a separate sheet, or make copies of this one.

Characteristic #1 _____
_____
_____

Characteristic #2 _____
_____
_____

Characteristic #3 _____
_____
_____

Characteristic #4 _____
_____
_____

Characteristic #5 _____
_____
_____

1. Define your target market

If I asked you to tell me who your customers—or potential customers—are, how would you answer?

Let's say you've created a new breakfast cereal for children: "Yummy Tummy Oats." You've packed it with good things: vitamins, minerals, great nutrition. You figure you're going to wipe out the competition because every parent wants a nutritious breakfast for their child.

There's only one problem: who's your customer? Is it mom or dad pushing the grocery cart down the cereal aisle, comparing the nutrition information on the side of the box?

Or is it the end-user (the "consumer") of your product—the kid—who couldn't care less about nutrition but wants cereal that tastes sweet, has cartoon characters on the package, and toys inside?

Or is it the cereal buyer for the grocery store chain? He couldn't care less about nutrition or cartoon characters. His concerns are more down-to-earth: how much money you're going to spend on advertising, how quickly you'll replenish inventory, and whether you'll pay him a "stocking fee" to obtain shelf space. Parents and children aren't going to have a chance to buy or eat "Yummy Tummy Oats" if you don't meet the supermarket buyer's needs first.

On top of that, if you don't have your own sales and distribution force, you may first have to find a cereal distributor and convince them to carry your product.

The parent. The child. The store buyer. The distributor. That's a lot of "customers" you have to satisfy with each box of "Yummy Tummy Oats."

You give yourself a competitive edge by thinking of each of these "customers" and planning for their needs and motivation.

Being responsive to the details that are important to distributors, retailers, sales representatives, and others helps you plan your marketing materials, operations, packaging, even the nature of the product itself. If yours is an industry where sales reps must purchase their samples, for instance, you can set yourself apart by supplying samples free. If retailers can fit more square packages on a shelf than round packages, you'll be more competitive by choosing a square package.

Even if you think you'll market "directly to consumers" on the Internet, you'll discover there are still many entities between you and your "customer" in cyberspace. In the case of "Yummy Tummy Oats," your intermediary might be the online grocery store, the health food site, the children's site, or the search engine that will help customers find you. So you'll still have more than just parents and kids to please.

As you begin to define your customers, both the end-users and the intermediaries, describe all of their various attributes: age, location, industry, purchasing patterns, buying sensitivities, "psychographics" (what motivates them), etc. Be realistic about how people actually behave—not how they should behave.

Use the worksheets on pages 57 and 58 to describe your customers. The first worksheet allows you to consider the types of "customers" you have. The second worksheet gets you started describing the characteristics of each of those. You may need to make copies of the customer profile worksheet—one for each type of "customer."

2. Determine if there are enough customers

Ever wonder why there seems to be three or four fast-food joints at the same intersection? Or why all of a sudden, not one but three big office supply stores open in a community?

The answer is they all rely on similar statistics to analyze a market. They look for certain factors: population density, characteristics of nearby residents (age, gender, income), number and type of local businesses, etc.

Big corporations hire consulting firms to compile these statistics. You've got an even bigger consulting group doing it for you—free! The UK Government, through the National Archive (www.nationalarchives.gov.uk), compiles all kinds of information useful for businesses, and they've put much of it on the Internet.

As you compile data on the size of your market, fill in the worksheet on page 61.

SIZE OF MY MARKET

Examine whether the market is large enough to bring you sufficient sales.

Estimated size of my market: _____

Is this number growing or declining? _____

By what amount per year? _____

Estimated number of competitors in my market: _____

Is this number growing or declining? _____

By what amount per year? _____

Realistic assessment of the opportunity for additional competitors in my market:

☐ Outstanding   ☐ Good   ☐ Moderate   ☐ Poor

ACCOMPLISHMENT #3:

Check out your competition

Tasks:

☐ **1. Identify your competitors**

☐ **2. Analyze your competition**

☐ **3. Compare competitors' pricing**

1. Identify your competitors

In general, I'm not a big believer in spending much time or energy worrying about what the other guy is doing. Over the years, I've learned that success for a small business depends much more on what you do, rather than on what your competitors are doing.

Yes, big businesses spend millions of pounds fighting over each percentage point of market share (just think Coke versus Pepsi, Ford versus GM). But for a small company, that's not very productive.

But that doesn't mean you can just ignore the competition. From time-to-time, you should check out who's out there, what they're offering, and what they're charging.

If you approach this competitive analysis exercise as an opportunity to learn, you may find ways to enhance your products or services, or at least improve your marketing.

Competition comes in three major forms:

1. **Direct competitors:** The ones who keep you up at night. They're other small companies like yours: close to customers, ambitious, and trying to reach the same target market. In most markets, there's enough business to go around, but you better know what your direct competition is doing.

2. **The Big Guys:** Asda, B&Q, Lawyers 'R' Us—national companies or franchises with huge marketing budgets. Don't just dismiss these as being inferior because they're big—a lot of them have adopted customer service practices that used to be the hallmark of small business. These are very real competitors to you, especially if you plan to compete on the basis of price.

3. **Alternatives and Inertia:** All the other ways a customer can spend their time and money. I can remodel my kitchen or go on a vacation; have a pedicure or buy a blouse. There are a million different ways I can spend my money. As a new business, you don't have the marketing pounds to compete against this kind of nebulous competition.

In most situations, you're going to concentrate your energy on looking at what your direct competitors are doing—who they are, what their competitive strengths and weaknesses are, and how much they charge.

You can identify these direct competitors by looking at directories (Yellow Pages, online directories, trade association directories, etc.) and advertisements. You can also ask suppliers and distributors to name the major competition in your area. Look to see if your competitors are exhibiting at trade shows. And you can do a survey of potential customers, asking them to name your competition.

2. Analyze your competition

"Let's go shopping!" While those are three of my favourite words, this spree is limited: we're going to check out what the competition is up to.

The easiest way to begin your competitive analysis is from the comfort of your computer. Just jump on the Internet. Here's the plan-of-attack:

1. **Direct competitors' websites:** Drill down way beyond the home page. Be sure to read the "About Us" section and any press information, as well as descriptions of their products or services.

   Here are some of the things to look for on your competitors' sites:

   ▪ **descriptions of products/services**
   ▪ **prices**

MY COMPETITORS

Use this worksheet to identify your competitors. What businesses compete with you directly? What other forces influence how or if your customers will spend their money on your product or service? Be realistic and honest in this assessment—it will help you build a better business and give you a competitive edge.

Competitor	Their Advantages/Strengths	My Advantages/Strengths

Direct Competitors:

_____   _____   _____

_____   _____   _____

_____   _____   _____

_____   _____   _____

Internet Based Competitors:

_____   _____   _____

_____   _____   _____

_____   _____   _____

Other Ways to Spend Money:

_____   _____   _____

_____   _____   _____

_____   _____   _____

Inertia Factors:

_____   _____   _____

_____   _____   _____

_____   _____   _____

Potential Future Competitors:

_____   _____   _____

_____   _____   _____

_____   _____   _____

_____   _____   _____

COMPETITORS' PRICE COMPARISON CHART

	Product/Service #1	Product/Service #2	Product/Service #3
Competitor A			
Competitor's price:			
Competitor's costs (if known):			
Basis for competitor's advantage (if any):			

Competitor B			
Competitor's price:			
Competitor's costs (if known):			
Basis for competitor's advantage (if any):			

Competitor C			
Competitor's price:			
Competitor's costs (if known):			
Basis for competitor's advantage (if any):			

- client/customer lists—testimonials
- staff—to see what size company they have and their qualifications
- their strengths
- how they position themselves—self-descriptions
- which segment of the market they appear to be targeting

2. **Next, try this trick to find which websites link to your competitors' websites:** Go to Google, www.Google.co.uk, and in their search box, type in the word "link," followed by a colon, then the full URL of the website (minus the http://). In other words, if I wanted to see who was linking to my website, I'd type "link:www.planningshop. com" to see who sends web traffic my way. You might then want to contact some of the websites that link to your competitors and ask them to link to you as well.

3. **You can also see if any of your competitors have been written about in the press** recently by checking their names at the Google News directory. Go to http://news.google.com.

4. **Going back to the Google home page,** do searches on the names of your competitors and the generic description of your product/ service category and location (if appropriate). Use alternative phrases as well. In other words, if you want to find out who's competing with you in the landscape business in Sherborne, also try phrases like "lawn care" and Dorset. Go also to the Yahoo directory, www.Yahoo. com.

5. **If you target specific industries as customers, check out the web-sites of those industry associations.** Search for listings of exhibitors at past trade shows (you might need to check under "events" or "conventions"). That will give you an idea of whether your competitors are actively marketing to the same industry.

6. **If you're willing to spend a bit of money,** and your competitors are pretty well established, you can get a Dun & Bradstreet report on them. Go to www.dnb.com. This highly-regarded agency was designed to help businesses check on the credit-worthiness of potential business customers. But it also gives you the opportunity to purchase a report containing financial and credit information about your competitors.

Finally, not all competitive analysis can be done online. Check to see if your competitors advertise in the newspaper or local Yellow Pages. You might phone or visit a competitor to see what they offer and how much they charge. Don't request proposals or bids—just ask for a simple brochure or have a quick discussion on the phone. Better yet, join a local branch of your trade association and get to know your competitors personally. Then, you can sit down and discuss what they're doing face-to-face. You may be surprised to find that some are actually helpful—and even a source of potential referrals!

In the best of all possible worlds, the fact you have competition should cause you to constantly improve your products and services. That way, you'll make more money—and can really go shopping!

Use the worksheet "My Competitors" on page 65 to identify and assess your competitors.

3. Compare competitors' pricing

One of the most important things you'll want to know when gathering data on your competition is to find out what they charge. After all, setting prices is one of the most difficult aspects of starting a new business. This is especially true in service industries, where prices can vary greatly from one provider to another.

Of course, finding out what others charge is not always easy. If you're lucky, they post their prices directly on their websites or in their written material.

In other cases, such as when you're opening a retail store or restaurant, your competitors' prices are visible when you go into their place of business. Just visiting their store enables you to check their prices.

Unfortunately, it's much more difficult to determine pricing patterns in professions and trades where prices are set on a one-on-one basis or negotiated. In these situations, you're more likely to find out about pricing patterns by asking others already in the field, talking to potential clients, and by participating in trade associations. In some cases, you may be able to speak with customers of other businesses in your industry about pricing.

Keep track of the information you find about competitors' pricing patterns on the worksheet on page 66.

Find suppliers

If you're opening a toy shop, how do you find the toys to put on your shelves? On the other hand, if you're manufacturing toys, how do you get your toys to be on those shelves?

In the business world, whether you're buying or selling, you're likely to need a "middle man"—a person or company that can put buyers and sellers together. While "middle men" may be much maligned, in reality they serve very valuable functions.

With the advent of the Internet, the business world was supposed to become "dis-intermediated;" in other words, we were supposed to be able to get rid of the middle man. Now, after all, manufacturers are able to sell directly to end users, without the need for all those people in the middle—wholesalers, distributors, retailers, and others. Theoretically, this should make everything less expensive because there would be fewer hands taking a cut, making a profit, at each step of the way.

But while this dis-intermediation has occurred in a few instances (buying a Dell computer directly from Dell), for the most part, manufacturers don't want to be bothered with selling goods on a "one-off" basis, then having to deal with fulfilling small orders and all those pesky customers. And buyers don't want to wade through dozens—even hundreds or thousands—of choices.

No, we need middle men: wholesalers, distributors, and independent sales representatives. They serve manufacturers by being the marketing, sales, and service arm for their businesses.

In turn, middle men also serve buyers by being an "editor" (selecting the best choices from the myriad of options), and providing individualised service and order fulfillment, especially for smaller customers.

But if you're new to business, where do you find these valuable intermediaries and vendors?

- **Word-of-mouth:** The best way to find a supplier or distributor is the old-fashioned way—asking someone who's knowledgeable for a recommendation. When I first started my publishing company, I asked another publisher for names of book distributors and printers. I didn't use their distributor, but their printing company is still my primary vendor to this day.

  If you don't know anyone in the same industry, ask others in related industries (for instance, ask a printer for the names of graphic designers or vice-versa) or those who might have a similar need (such as for shipping services or sign painters).

- **Trade associations:** Trade associations are an excellent source for locating suppliers. Besides holding annual or regional conventions and trade shows where suppliers exhibit their products and services, many associations publish supplier directories, both in print and online. Use the methods listed in the section "Learn more about your industry" to find an association serving your industry.

- **Yahoo! business-to-business (B2B) directory:** Most online directories maintain separate categories for business-related topics. Yahoo, as one of the oldest directories, has an extensive list. You can find it at http://dir.yahoo.com/Business_and_Economy/Business_to_Business/.

POTENTIAL STRATEGIC PARTNERS

Use this space to start a list of potential strategic partners, how you can help each other,
and how you can secure a relationship with them.

Potential Strategic Partners	Mutual Benefits	Ways to Start a Relationship

ACCOMPLISHMENT #5:

Consider strategic partners

You don't have to do everything alone. A strategic partnership is a relationship with another company for purposes such as distribution, product development, promotion, or add-on sales. A strong strategic partner that is already serving your target market can give you a real edge in reaching that market.

For example, you might use a partnership for:

- **Distribution agreement:** This is an agreement whereby one company carries another's product line and sells its products or services. This is the most common type of strategic partnership.

- **Licensing:** One company may grant permission to another to use its product, name, or trademark. Instead of selling your product or service directly, you might license it to another company to sell under its name and brand. Examples abound in the entertainment industry where, for instance, toy manufacturers will license a movie's brand and create toys around the movie's main characters. Professional atheletes often also license their likenesses for promoting consumer goods.

- **Cooperative advertising:** This type of advertising occurs when two companies are mentioned in an advertisement and each company pays part of the costs. This is a frequent practice in many industries. Start with your trade association when looking for such opportunities. Manufacturers also often put together co-op advertising packages for their distributors and retailers.

- **Bundling:** This is a relationship between two companies where one company includes another company's product or service as part of a total package. You keep your own identity, but get the advantage of being included in their package.

Securing a major company as a key partner can not only give your company specific competitive advantages, but also credibility with customers and funders.

Use the worksheet "Potential Strategic Partners" on page 71 to identify those with whom you might form a strategic partnership in which you both benefit.

ACCOMPLISHMENT #6:
Broaden/establish your network

Tasks:

☐ 1. **Attend a community, entrepreneur, or industry organisation meeting**

There's one piece of advice I always give entrepreneurs as they're starting out in business: join an organisation. You can't build a company if you're sitting in your office by yourself; you need to be part of a community or an industry, or better yet, both.

Since I began my business, I've participated in many groups—entrepreneurs' clubs, industry associations, women's business groups, local chambers of commerce, and more. I've never sat down and figured out how much I've spent on memberships, meetings, and meals, but I'm sure it adds up to quite a sum. And I can say, without a doubt, it's been worth every penny.

After all, it was at a referrals group that I first learned how to give an "elevator pitch" (the short description of my services). That's where I found many of my clients during my early years in business. In fact, it was through someone at an entrepreneurs' group that I made the connection that led to my first book contract. And that changed my life!

Entrepreneurs are even more fortunate now. There are many more resources to help you launch your business, learn your industry, and make important contacts than when I was starting my company.

What will you get out of joining an organisation?

- **Community:** Working alone or in a very small business, it's easy to feel isolated. Joining organisations helps you become part of a larger community.

- **Connections:** If you're looking for the name of an attorney or graphic artist, trying to find a supplier, or just need advice on how to handle a problem or price your services, you'll have connections to others with experience.

- **Education:** Many groups, especially entrepreneur and industry associations, provide valuable information and training. They can help you stay on top of current trends.

- **Friends:** You can meet people who become your personal friends, regardless of any business connection or benefit.

- **New business:** Of course, it's ideal if you get clients or referrals as a result of joining an organisation. But I should warn you, if that's your only goal, you're likely to drop out fairly quickly.

Every community has its share of organisations. Some types of groups you can join:

- **Entrepreneurs' groups:** You're likely to find lots of entrepreneur groups, both formal associations and informal get-togethers. Don't forget the grand-daddy of them all—the Chamber of Commerce.

- **Industry associations:** With industry and professional associations covering just about every conceivable field of commerce it's likely that there's a local group of interest in your community.

- **Group-specific entrepreneur associations:** You'll find business organisations aimed at women, minorities, religious groups, gays, youth, immigrants, and more.

- **Civic organisations:** In big cities, you'll find organisations dedicated to civic or world affairs, politics, etc. You're certain to find service groups such as Rotary International, Kiwanis, Lions Clubs in your town. Established business leaders are more likely to belong to civic organisations than to entrepreneur groups.

Check the following to find out if there's a group that's right for you in your town:

- **Business section** of your local newspaper for calendar of meetings/ events of entrepreneur groups.

- **Community calendar** of your local newspaper for civic organisations.

ORGANISATIONS TO JOIN

Use this worksheet to keep information about networking, trade, business, charity, and social organisations you will join or in which you will participate.

Organisation	Meeting Time & Place	Dues

- **Websites of trade associations.** Find an appropriate industry association by using the methods in the section "Learn more about your industry."

- **Chambers of Commerce directory** online, www.uschamber.com/chambers/chamber_directory.asp.

- **Websites of women's groups,** particularly National Association of Women's Business Owners (www.nawbo.org) and Forum for Women Entrepreneurs (www.fwe.org).

- **Websites of civic organisations.** Check an Internet directory, such as Yahoo!'s directory of community organisations, or the site of the specific group, e.g., www.rotary.org or www.kiwanis.org.

Finally, consider joining an online group. There are literally thousands of free and for-a-fee "virtual" forums on the Internet where entrepreneurs congregate to discuss issues and ideas surrounding their particular industry. These groups can be great sources of information on suppliers and vendors, best practices, educational opportunities, etc. Post a specific question and receive credible answers from people "who have been there"—sometimes in just a matter of hours. In some cases, you'll find you're hobnobbing with the top names in your industry!

Keep in mind, however, that just as in the "real" world, these forums typically have codes of conduct and generally-accepted rules of etiquette. Most, for instance, frown on blatant advertising of one's business or products. It's always a good policy to spend a week or two "lurking"—reading other participants' postings, learning who's who, getting the lay of the land—before you venture in with your own postings.

Also, as with the real world, consider the source before you apply anyone's advice to your business. While most forums I've participated in have been good sources of information and camaraderie, the Internet unfortunately provides an accommodating home for both unscrupulous people and plenty who, innocently enough, just offer poor advice.

There are undoubtedly many ways to find online forums; here are some good places to start your search:

- **Your industry association website:** Many associations run members-only forums on their websites, and this is the first place to look for a forum that will be useful to you. If your industry association offers such a service, sign up and jump in. If not, suggest they start one.

- **Yahoo! Groups** (http://groups.yahoo.com): Yahoo hosts all sorts of online groups. Many are for people with particular interests, hobbies, health concerns, etc. But there are professional groups also, so spend some time looking around for one that fits your business type.

- **Google Groups** (http://groups.google.com): Everyone loves Google's search engine, but the company is also host to one of the Internet's largest and oldest repositories of online forums. You'll find discussion groups on just about every topic under the sun. Spend some time on the Groups home page looking for topic areas that relate to your industry or business specialty.

1. Attend a community, entrepreneur, or industry organisation meeting

If you want to get the most out of an organisation, don't just go to one or two meetings; attend regularly, volunteer, serve on a committee. That's how people will get to know you, and both you and the organisation will be more likely to succeed.

So this week, get out there and mingle! I'm suggesting you attend just one event—but if you're feeling ambitious, by all means, attend two, or even three. The most important thing is to face that fear of meeting new people—a fear that most everyone has—and to take the plunge. No matter what type of business you're starting, chances are you'll need to be prepared to meet and converse with new people. So start now!

Use the worksheet on page 75 to keep track of organisations you'll join.

week 3

week 3

CUT THROUGH RED TAPE

Main accomplishments:
- ✓ Deal with legal and licensing matters
- ✓ Build your team and employee structure

Make appointments with:
- ✓ Lawyer

cut throug

red tape

Yuck! No one enjoys dealing with the red tape—the paperwork and legal requirements—of starting and running a business. But, unfortunately, it has to be done, so this week we're going to get it out of the way.

The key activity is meeting with a solicitor or accountant. The UK is possibly unique in its determination to view accountants as general business advisors on start-up business, and most banks will have small business advisors available as well.

If yours is a simple business, this may all go pretty quickly. But even if yours is a one-person business and you work out of your home, don't think you can just forego the legal issues altogether. An ounce of legal prevention now can prevent a ton of legal trouble later.

Aside from dealing with legal issues, this week you'll get started on building your team. Taking advantage of the time you spend with an advisor, you can ask for advice on personnel matters: hiring, benefits, taxes, and other issues to make sure you follow the law, and then hire the right people, treat them fairly, and manage them well.

You'll also plan who you need on your team, including what kind of advisors you may want or need. You can even get the hiring process underway!

ACCOMPLISHMENT #1:

Deal with legal and licensing matters

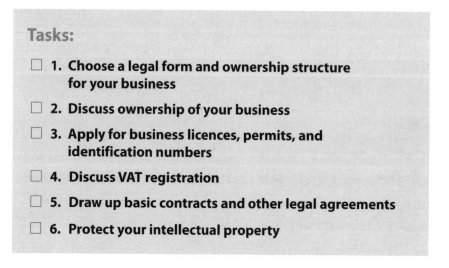

Tasks:

☐ 1. **Choose a legal form and ownership structure for your business**

☐ 2. **Discuss ownership of your business**

☐ 3. **Apply for business licences, permits, and identification numbers**

☐ 4. **Discuss VAT registration**

☐ 5. **Draw up basic contracts and other legal agreements**

☐ 6. **Protect your intellectual property**

The origin of the term "Red Tape"
In England, at least as far back as the 17th century, stacks of legal documents were tied in red cloth ribbon. By the 19th century, "red tape" had come to connote any kind of bureaucratic or legal complication.

Taking care of your company's legal health is like taking care of your personal health: an ounce of prevention is better than a pound of cure. Time after time, entrepreneurs end up in legal battles costing thousands of pounds that could have been avoided with a £200 trip to a specialist.

Make your first visit to an accountant at the beginning of your business life. Look for an expert who handles general business law, especially with new or small companies. Ideally, he or she will have experience with companies in your industry, but that is certainly not necessary unless you are in an industry that is highly regulated. The best way to find the right person is by asking for referrals, especially from others in your field.

When I went in to business for the first time with my own consulting practice, I spent two hours with a lawyer. We not only wrote a simple letter-of-agreement I could use with clients, but we also discussed how to price my services, collect overdue fees, and minimise taxes.

Accountants' costs vary, but some have set fees for specific tasks such as incorporation. Don't hesitate to interview your prospective accountant and ask about costs before engaging their services. You have the right to choose someone you're comfortable with and can afford. Then, establish a good working relationship with a business lawyer and become used to consulting with them before you make major business decisions.

In addition to making that vital trip to a specialist's office, you can also consult a number of other resources to help you with legal and licensing issues. These include:

- **Business Link** (see page 25): Your local Business Link office is likely to be able to help you understand the specific business regulations you'll have to deal with in your community.

- **BusinessLaw:** http://www.bizhelp24.com/business-law/2.html is a private site (as distinct from a Government site) built to link business-people to all manner of legal documentation and regulatory information. At the time of writing this book it appeared comprehensive and accurate – although it's always worth double-checking anything you might find on the web from an unknown source.

- **Individual County Council websites:** Many council websites will have information for businesses in their area. Unfortunately there's no standard form for a council website so it's a matter of either Googling for the website or trying www.yourlocalauthorityname.gov.uk and clicking any likely-looking links from there.

1. Choose a legal form and ownership structure for your company

When starting a business, one of the first questions you need to answer is what kind of legal form your business will take.

Now, this may sound like a question that shouldn't be important to a very small business. After all, if you're going to be a consultant or a graphic designer or an electrical contractor, why bother dealing with the government? Who needs to pay a few hundred pounds in corporation or legal fees?

But choosing a legal form affects how much you pay in taxes, who can invest in your company, and most importantly, your personal financial security.

Three things to keep in mind when choosing a legal form are:

- **Liability:** Legally, corporations are considered individual entities. As such, the corporation—not individual shareholders—are responsible

FORMS OF BUSINESS ORGANISATION COMPARED

Legal Form	What Is It?	Advantages?
Sole trader	A business owned by one person that is not incorporated or an LLC. If you don't set up any other legal structure, and no one else owns any part of your business, you are a sole trader.	Simple. No legal forms or costs to establish. No "double taxation."
General partnership	A business with more than one owner in which all partners actively participate in the business.	You have the time and talents of more than one person. No double taxation.
Limited Liability Partnership (LLP)	A legal form which provides much of the protection of incorporating with most of the simplicity of a sole proprietorship.	Protects your personal assets against most business losses. No double taxation. Relatively simple, inexpensive to establish and maintain. Can distribute profits and losses disproportionately to ownership interest.
Limited Liability Company (LLC)	A step more formal than limted liability partnership. There are shareholders rather than partners and these shareholders appoint directors. They have no financial obligation beyond the money they put in initially. The essential point is that, unlike a partnership, a limited company exists in its own right as a legal entity.	Protects personal assets and offers a firm framework recognised in law.

for the actions of the business. In other words, if something goes very wrong and a corporation is sued, only the assets of the corporation are at stake—not the owners' personal assets. (There are some exceptions to this rule, but generally, your personal liability is *greatly* limited.) Obviously, having liability limited to the company's assets is quite desirable, since it means your personal assets—your home, investments, savings—can't be seized if your company has a legal judgment against it.

■ **Double taxation:** No one likes paying taxes, and you certainly don't want to pay taxes twice—once on income for the business and then again when that income is distributed as profits to you. Instead, look for a legal form that allows for the profits of the company to "pass

FORMS OF BUSINESS ORGANISATION COMPARED

Disadvantages?	Tax Treatment	Watch Out For
Provides no protection of personal assets from business losses. The business owner has unlimited personal liability for the debts, obligations, and judgments against the company. The business owner's spouse may likewise be liable.	"Pass through" profits and losses, so the business owner can deduct losses against other personal income, and there is no "double taxation."	In community property states, spouses may be liable for business debts as well as having an ownership interest in the company.
Each partner has unlimited personal liability for business losses or obligations. Each partner can sign contracts and incur debts that all partners are liable for.	"Pass through" profits and losses to the partners who pay tax at their individual rates. Partnership pays no corporation tax.	If you go into business with other people, you have a partnership whether you draw up documents or not, and they will have a share of the business and other legal rights.
Each owner can enter into contracts and incur debts for the entire LLP.	"Pass through" profits and losses to each owner.	Be sure to have a written agreement spelling out the percentage ownership of each member to avoid confusion or conflict later.
Rigid reporting requirements such as annual returns might put some people off, although if you're having those doubts you might well ask whether running a business is for you.	Corporation tax applies and once shareholders are paid their dividend it goes on to their self-assessment tax form at the end of the year and may be taxed again.	Overstated claims that personal assets are protected. True though this is technically, if you're looking for financing from (say) the bank you're almost certainly going to have to put personal assets like your home up for security.

through" to the owners, without having to pay corporate taxes first.

When you meet with your accountant or lawyer, these are the legal structures you can consider:

- **Sole trader:** A business owned by one person with no formal legal structure. ADVANTAGES: It's simple! Just start your business; there's no additional paperwork. You don't file corporate income taxes—just a Schedule D for National Insurance with your personal income taxes. DISADVANTAGES: You have no personal liability protection. If your business is sued, you could lose everything you own—and in some cases, your spouse could lose his or her assets also.

- **Partnership:** A business with more than one owner who actively engages in the management of the company. ADVANTAGES: No required legal forms (although you'd be well advised to draw up a partnership agreement). No double taxation—profits pass through to the partners. DISADVANTAGES: Each partner has unlimited personal liability, even for actions taken by other partners. Be warned: if you go into business with others, you've got a partnership in the eyes of the law whether or not you've drawn up any paperwork.

- **Limited Liability Partnership (LLP):** A legal form which provides much of the protection of incorporating with most of the simplicity of a sole proprietorship. ADVANTAGES: protects your personal assets against most business losses. No double taxation. Relatively simple, inexpensive to establish and maintain. Can distribute profits and losses disproportionately to ownership interest. DISADVANTAGES: each owner can enter into contracts and incur debts for the entire LLP.

- **Limited Liability Company (LLC):** AA step more formal than limted liability partnership. There are shareholders rather than partners and these shareholders appoint directors. They have no financial obligation beyond the money they put in initially. The essential point is that, unlike a partnership, a limited company exists in its own right as a legal entity. ADVANTAGES: protects personal assets and offers a firm framework recognised in law.. DISADVANTAGES: rigid reporting requirements such as annual returns.

There is one other form of company—a "non-profit corporation"—for organisations that are formed for the public benefit, such as schools and philanthropic agencies.

A chart outlining the pros and cons of the different types of legal entities is included on pages 84–85.

2. Discuss ownership of your company

One of the key issues involved in choosing a legal form for your business is determining who owns it. In a sole proprietorship, you own it. In any other form, you share ownership, either with a partner or shareholders.

If this is your first time in business, you may imagine that you can get someone to invest in your company and then leave you completely alone. Wouldn't that be nice! The truth is, when someone invests in your company, they become a part-owner. And the minute someone owns a piece of your company, they acquire certain rights.

Some forms of ownership give investors more rights than others. Also, if you haven't set up either a corporation, LLC, or limited partnership, your investors are also likely to become legally responsible for your company's debts.

You may also think you're protected from other shareholders meddling in the business as long as you keep more than 50% ownership in the company. Beware: depending on your corporate form, whether you have a board of directors, and other factors, shareholders not only have rights, they make binding decisions for the company, and can even remove you from management.

Before you begin parting with any ownership interest in your company—even taking on a good friend or family member as partner—discuss the ramifications with your accountant or lawyer.

Issuing stock

In the early days of your company, when you have very limited money, you may be tempted to promise or hand out a small share of ownership to anyone who invests money in your company or provides you with products or services. After all, it seems a lot cheaper to pay someone with stock than with cash. And it seems a promising sign that others feel that stock in your company will be worth something some day.

RED TAPE ALERT!

Any time you deal with stock in your company, you face a host of potential legal and tax implications. Be very cautious about distributing or promising stock in your company and don't do it before you've discussed it thoroughly with a competent lawyer and accountant! If, for instance, in the early days of your company, you give a consultant an amount of stock in return for a certain monetary value of service (e.g., 10,000 shares of stock for £5,000 worth of graphic design work), you may inadvertently be placing a value on all other stock that the company has issued or will issue, including the stock you and other founders own. This can have a significant tax impact on you and others. If you are issuing stock to company founders, or stock options to employees, be sure the correct paperwork, including a "Form 83B Election," has been done, or you may all incur significantly higher taxes.

PEOPLE YOU'VE GIVEN OR PROMISED STOCK

Use this space to keep track of people to whom you've given or promised stock. When starting a new company, you may use promises of stock in many ways—from raising venture money to getting your logo designed. Discuss with your lawyer how to draw up these formal agreements.

Name	Amount or Value of Stock

STOCK DISTRIBUTION PLAN

What percentage of the company do you want or need to give to others? In a young company, the number of shares is not as important as the percentage ownership those shares represent. Use this worksheet to plan the distribution of stock in your company.

	Number of Shares	Percent of Ownership	Vesting Period
Founder #1			
Founder #2			
Founder #3			
CEO			
Chief Operating Officer			
Chief Technology Officer			
Chief Financial Officer			
Other Officer level employees			
VP level employees			
Director level employees			
Manager level employees			
Other long-time or key employees			
Other employee levels			
Investors			
Consultants/Professional Service firms			
Advisory Committee Members			
Board of Directors Members			
Strategic Partners			
Others			

Anytime you issue stock, you have legal and financial considerations to deal with. Moreover, you're also diluting your own ownership of the company. When you give someone stock, they're getting a "share" of the company and a percentage of the ownership.

Corporations—not sole proprietorships or LLCs—are the only legal entities that can issue stock. For an LLC, instead of stock, you spell out what percent of ownership each partner/investor receives in the LLC documents. Corporations, however, can not only issue stock, they can issue different classes of stock—preferred or common—with some shareholders getting better financial treatment than others. For instance, preferred stock shareholders may get paid before common stock shareholders if the company closes and remaining assets are distributed.

If you decide you're going to issue stock in your company, before you start making promises of stock to anyone else, come up with a "Stock Distribution Plan." Investors, of course, will take a significant piece of the ownership, as will you and any other company founders. Set aside a pool of stock for key employees you're going to recruit in the future and all other employees. You may also choose to give stock to consultants or other service providers, as well as granting stock to your advisory committee members, strategic partners, and others.

Decide at what point a person's stock "vests" or actually becomes theirs. Because your goal is to have good employees stay with the business, you typically want their stock to vest over a period of years. If you set up a four-year vesting period, for example, employees might be entitled to one-fourth of their stock after the first year, and then another 1/48th of their stock each month (4 years times 12 months). That way, if they leave before their stock vests, they don't receive more than they deserve.

Use the worksheets on the previous pages to outline your stock distribution plan and keep track of whom you've promised or given stock.

3. Apply for business licences, permits, and identification numbers

Whoa! You may be ready to start your business, but the authorities may not want you to—at least not without making sure you have the proper licences or permits. As frustrating as it may seem, you can't just rent an office or a store and set up shop.

BUSINESS LICENCES & PERMITS

List the licences and permits you need, including where and how to apply, requirements and fees.

Licence Type	Agency & Contact Info	Requirements	Fees
Local Licences:			
Local Permits:			
County Licences/ Permits:			
DBA required:			
Other:			

The bureaucratic things you'll deal with fall into three general categories:

1. **Identification numbers:** to keep track of your business with government authorities. Example: identification numbers for income tax purposes.

2. **Licences (or certifications):** required to engage in any business or certain types of businesses or professions. Examples: a city business licence, a contractor's licence, licence to sell alcoholic beverages, an optometrist certification.

3. **Permits:** required for particular, often more limited, actions. Examples: construction permits, special event permits.

Sometimes, these terms are used interchangeably, such as "permit" instead of "licence" or vice versa.

The requirements may vary depending on the type of business you're opening and any local regulations where you want to do business. For example, an entrepreneur might notice there are no pubs in a certain area of London SW17, locally known as Furzedown; a lawyer would find out that this isn't because nobody has thought of it but because the previous land owner from centuries ago, Lord Furzedown, managed to put it in the local regulations that there should never be such an establishment on his land. That's why it's good to ask a lawyer about these types of licences.

Listed below are some of the most common issues you're likely to deal with in getting permits, licences, and identification numbers.

Use the worksheet on the previous page to keep track of which licences and permits you'll need.

VITAL STATISTICS

Use this worksheet to keep track of those important dates, numbers and information about the legal status of your business or yourself. You may be asked to refer to these often.

Date of incorporation:	
Corporation number:	
Formal company name:	
Trading names:	
Company registration number:	
Business licence or permit/number:	
Business licence or permit/number:	
Business licence or permit/number:	
Other:	

Tax and company registration numbers

The registration numbers you'll need will depend on the sort of business you've started. Sole traders will need to register as such but the only compulsory red tape outside of keeping detailed records of income and expenditure is an extra page on their self-assessment tax form every year. Your own tax reference number is all you're likely to need until you start turning over more money.

Companies will need a company registration number which will be sent by Companies House when your accountant or lawyer registers your business. This goes onto a company tax return form alongside the company's tax reference number, shown on form CT603, which also comes automatically when a business is incorporated.

Trading name or fictitious business name

If you use any name other than your own personal name for doing business, you'll you'll want to use a trading name. HMRC wll keep only one of these names on file and you'll find your chequebook will say 'Fred Smith t/a Maggots inc.' if you sell fishing tackle, for example. This means your customer always knows who they're dealing with, and don't forget it's your job to make that clear.

In other words, if I own a flower shop called "Blooming Nuts" and haven't registered as a Limited Company (if I have, then Blooming Nuts becomes a legal entity in its own right and I am traceable as a director) then my cheque book will tell people I am Rhonda Abrams t/a Blooming Nuts.

Check with your lawyer or accountant – all of this can change when a new Government comes into office or whenever a new Chancellor of the Exchequer has nothing better to do on a rainy afternoon!

4. Registering for VAT

As a buyer, when I purchase something from a local business, I pay Value Added Tax (VAT). I may not like the extra cost, but it's a pretty seamless transaction—the seller just tacks on the appropriate percentage, and I pay the total amount. But what happens when I'm the seller?

How do you, as a businessperson, know whether you have to collect VAT? Here's the short answer: Immediately you turn over more than £64,000 in a 12-month period you must register for VAT and start charging it to your customers in almost every field. There are a number of exceptions: financial advisors may not register for VAT and neither may charities; children's clothing, books and a number of other items are zero rated but you can still register voluntarily.

The impact on a business that is well-run will be minimal as you'll have your records up to date anyway. Essentially you charge 17.5 per cent tax and send this income to the Government once a quarter after filling in a simple VAT return. The good thing is that you declare any VAT you might have paid and this is deducted from your bill. So if, say, you're a book publisher whose products are zero rated but you've spent £1175.00 on a computer including VAT, Her Majesty's Customs and Excise will refund you £175 as the VAT portion of whatever you've spent. This is why many businesses register for VAT regardless of whether they have reached the VAT threshold.

Should you opt not to do so, you might have an issue with your prices when you come to register compulsorily. If you are selling products and services to a business that's fine; prior to registration you sell them something for £1000; afterwards it costs them £1175 but they get the extra £175 back when they put their VAT return in.

Consumers, charities and businesses that are exempt from VAT will not be able to reclaim their VAT. This means that if you were selling to consumers and charging £10 for a T-shirt one week and then registered for VAT you'd either have to put your price up to £11.75 and the customer would have either to pay the extra or not buy from you any more, or put your retained price down so that £10 included VAT – this would mean the actual price you're charging goes down to £8.51, with £1.49 going to HMRC at the end of the financial quarter.

Bear this in mind when you're setting up your business and setting prices. It need not be a massive issue but it will catch you out and possible lose you some business if you overlook it and are selling to people who can't claim VAT back.

5. Draw up basic contracts and other legal agreements

While the days of doing business with just a handshake may not be over entirely, doing so leaves you at risk. Ours is becoming a litigious society, and the best way to avoid ending up in court—or in hot water—is to get things in writing.

You're likely to find you have a number of agreements or contracts that you you'll use over and over. For instance, a consultant may have a simple letter of engagement; an electrician might have a standard contract. Have your lawyer help you draft a standard template for these documents, into which you can just plug the specifics each time.

Some of the many types of legal agreements you may need include:

- **Contract**
- **Letter of agreement or engagement**
- **Leases**
- **Employment contracts**
- **Distribution agreements**
- **Project proposals**
- **Work-for-hire agreements**

6. Protect your intellectual property

What is the value of the Nike "swoosh?" The design of a Macintosh computer? The content of a Beatles song? We all recognise that these things have a value far beyond the "physical property" of the running shoes, computers, or CDs themselves because of the "intellectual property" of the swoosh, the design, or the wonderful music and lyrics of John Lennon and Paul McCartney.

Every company has certain intangible things that are, or can be, very valuable. Many of these come under the heading of "Intellectual Property"—assets that have value because of the knowledge, recognition, inventiveness, etc. that they consist of. Indeed, some companies *only* have products composed of intellectual property—software developers, writers, inventors, consultants, and many more.

So just as you would protect the physical property of your company, you need to protect your intellectual property.

Trade secrets: Just about every company has ideas or knowledge that gives them a competitive edge, and which would be harmful if shared with others. If you're just starting out, your business concept may be one of your major assets. But "trade secrets" covers a huge range of things— from how you make a product to the preferences of your best customer.

The law provides a certain amount of protection to you for your trade secrets—but only if you take steps to keep such information secret. So be careful how you disseminate information: mark documents "confidential," get others to sign non-disclosure agreements, put passwords and other security measures on "work-in-progress" websites or computer programs, and be careful who you talk to!

Non-disclosure agreements: One of the simplest ways to protect your ideas is to get a signed non-disclosure agreement or confidentiality agreement before discussing your concepts with others. This is a typical procedure, and you'll often be asked to sign NDAs if you're trying to do business with another company. Venture capitalists will *not* sign NDAs as they see too many new business ideas.

WHAT WOULD RHONDA DO?

TRADEMARKS

I'd be sure to avoid any name close to or potentially confusing with a big company's trademark. It may seem silly when a big corporation goes after a tiny company, but if a company doesn't protect their trademark, the law says they can lose it. They have no choice but to sue. Even if you're legally in the clear, with a trademark issued to you, the reality is that in trademark issues, the side with the greatest ability and willingness to spend money on lawyers gets their way. McDonald's, for instance, vigorously goes after any company that uses the prefix "Mc" even for products or services that could not possibly be confused with food. So don't even think of naming your barber shop "McHaircut."

Non-compete agreements: Once a trade secret is learned, it can't be unlearned. So sometimes the biggest fear you have is that a valuable and knowledgeable employee will go to work for a competitor. To help guard against this, you may want to have employees sign an agreement limiting their ability to go work for a competing company (or start their own competing company) for a period of time. Non-compete agreements provide a measure of protection, but courts don't like enforcing them, so make certain they are carefully written and appropriately used.

Copyrights: If you're creating works that others might want to copy—content, music, art, software, illustrations, etc.—you'll want to protect what you've created. This is where copyright law comes in.

Copyrights cover any type of work that is "fixed" and "tangible"—even if it's only computer code, words spoken on an audio tape, or images "fixed" on a movie.

Copyrights do not cover "ideas" no matter how unique, just the particular fixed expression of that idea. For instance, you can't copyright your idea to have a boy go off to a school for wizards, but you can copyright your novel telling the story of this boy.

Once you have a copyright, you retain the rights to that creation, and no one else can make a movie about your hero without your permission.

You also can't copyright "facts." So if what you're creating is purely the compilation of facts, you won't be able to copyright that.

Copyrights are easy to get. The rights to your creation are yours *at the moment you create it;* theoretically, you don't have to do anything to insure your copyright. But that's putting you at some risk. The easiest thing to do to protect your copyright is to add a simple copyright notice whenever you produce something. Just add the word "copyright," the © notice, the date, and your name.

RED TAPE ALERT! Whenever you have others help create any of your intellectual property, you want to make clear who owns what they develop. For instance, if you have a graphic designer create your logo, software developers write computer code, or writers create content, who owns the rights to all those creations? In most cases, you want to make sure you do! One business in Brighton came badly unstuck when it found, after falling out with its web design agency, that the agency owned the rights to its website so it was unable to update anything. This effectively paralysed the business until an agreement involving extra money was reached. So in your contract or agreement, clarify the ownership of the work product, make certain that they are required to transfer any copyright or other ownership if necessary, and specify that you are hiring them on a "work for hire" basis, with all work product becoming your property. And have the agreement looked at by a lawyer.

Patents: Copyrights are easy to get; patents are incredibly tough. Copyrights cost little; patents are very expensive. Copyrights are yours the instant you create the work; patents can take years to get issued. Patents are also difficult and costly to enforce—if someone violates your patent and starts selling a knock-off of your product, it may take a lot of money (in legal fees) and time to put a stop to it—and if they're overseas, enforcement will be even harder. So if you're building your business around a new invention, process, machine, recipe, or formula that needs to be patented, it's going to be tough going.

If, however, you have a new invention or a new process that is indeed unique, "non-obvious" (a requirement for qualifying for a patent), and worth a lot of money, then pursue the patent process. The first thing you'll need—after you've come up with your new invention or idea—is a good patent lawyer. A good one will warn you of the costs and pitfalls before you get too far down the road. To find a competent patent lawyer, start by asking your solicitor.

ACCOMPLISHMENT #2:

Build your team and personnel structure

Tasks:

- ☐ 1. **Consider your support structure**
- ☐ 2. **Decide who you need on your team**
- ☐ 3. **Examine the use of independent contractors**
- ☐ 4. **Understand employment laws and consider your personnel policies**
- ☐ 5. **Appraise your management style**

1. Consider your support structure

You don't have to have employees to build a team. Even if yours is a one-person business, you'll want to find people to turn to for guidance as you start, run, and grow your company. Building a company can be lonely work. Advisors can be one of the most valuable assets an entrepreneur can have, providing support, contacts, and advice.

Business buddies/Mentors: In my early years in business—when I worked alone and out of my home—I had what I called my "business buddy," Jennifer. Jennifer was a good friend who had started a consulting practice at about the same time I did. Her work was similar to mine, although in a different industry.

Jennifer and I would share templates for writing proposals or sending invoices. We'd discuss how to bill or collect from our clients and swap solutions to client problems we were having. Sometimes the most important thing was just to have a conversation in the middle of the afternoon when one of us felt lonely or overwhelmed.

Finding a novice entrepreneur who's in the same stage of business as you can be a great way to get support. You'll have each other to think through ideas, learn from, and be each other's cheerleader.

MY SUPPORT SYSTEM

Use this worksheet to list the names or sources of people or organisations you can turn to for support and advice. You may list people who have already committed to supporting you, or list potential supporters you want to ask for help in the future.

Business buddies:

Mentors:

Entrepreneurs' groups:

Industry groups:

Advisory committee members:

Board members:

Others:

If you can, you might want to find a more experienced businessperson to serve as your informal "mentor." Many accomplished entrepreneurs enjoy helping others, and you can learn from someone who's already gone through the process of setting up a business.

Don't be afraid to ask for help. Many people are willing to be of assistance, especially if you're professional in your approach and realistic about what kind of help you need and wthat they're able to offer.

Advisory Committee: An Advisory Committee is an informal group with no legal authority, no legal liability, and no set rules about when to meet or how many people must be involved. In fact, they don't ever have to meet; your advisory committee can simply be a few people who've agreed to let you turn to them for advice.

The point of having advisors is to seek advice, so look for people whose advice you trust to serve on your committee. Ideally you'll find wise folks who are seasoned entrepreneurs from your industry. Be wary of asking potential investors, customers, employees, or, naturally, competitors. You don't need many advisors, and you don't have to ask everybody at once.

Most people willing to be an advisor aren't motivated by money—they're motivated to help you succeed. If you do want to reward them, and you're setting up stock in your company, granting stock would be a good form of compensation; that way, your advisors will share in your success. Of course, make sure your advisors get any company trinkets—t-shirts, coffee mugs, pens, etc.

One of the best things about formally asking people to serve as members of your "Advisory Committee" is that they then have a sense of ownership and continuing interest in your company. They may initiate conversations with you, make suggestions, provide useful connections. Setting up an Advisory Committee is a good way to get support from people you trust and admire.

Board of Directors: This is typically a legal entity required for an incorporated company. A Board has legal responsibilities established by the state and will probably be required to meet at least once a year and record minutes of their meetings.

Members of the Board of Directors have a fiduciary duty to protect the interests of the shareholders of the company—not to protect you. They can control the decisions about management of the company even if you own a controlling interest in the stock. They have legal liability for the company's actions, so they should take their role very seriously. In many companies, especially large companies, Board members are paid—or at least reimbursed for their expenses incurred coming to Board meetings or doing company business.

You may not need to have any members of the Board other than yourself or the company owners/founders and you may not need any outside Board members. But there are occasions when you might want to—or need to—invite outside people to sit on your Board. For instance, if you have investors, especially venture capitalists, they'll expect to be on the Board. If you are able to secure well-known individuals from your industry, or a related industry, you can gain valuable advice and insight as well as adding stature and connections to your company.

Who should you ask to be on your Board? Since the Board makes legally-binding decisions for the company, be very careful about whom you ask. The best Board members are those who understand your business, are supportive of you (even when they challenge particular decisions), have a long-range view of your company's growth, and bring excellent connections to the business or financial world.

Use the worksheet on page 101 to sketch out how you'll build your support system.

2. Decide who you need on your team

Who is important to your company's success? Who will handle your financial affairs, make sales, plan operations, produce your goods? What roles do you need to fill "in-house" and what jobs can you fill with outside contractors or suppliers? Who can you turn to for advice?

Every company's need for staff is unique—a restaurant clearly has different demands for employees than a sporting goods store, and a medical equipment manufacturer requires a very different staffing arrangement than a consulting firm.

Some companies—such as consulting firms—can be more flexible in their hiring arrangements, perhaps only hiring employees or using independent contractors after a client or project is secured. Others—such as manufacturers—usually need staff before they actually can make a sale.

WHO DO I NEED ON MY TEAM?

List the job titles needed in each area. Some suggestions for managers and officers are in parentheses, but you should hire only those your company really needs as it grows.

Key Personnel	Responsibilities	Desired Experience/Background
Top Management (President/CEO)		
Administrative (Chief Operating Officer)		
Financial (Chief Financial Officer, Controller, bookkeeper, etc.)		
Marketing/Sales/PR (VP Marketing, Director of Sales, PR Director)		
Operations/Production (Production Manager, Inventory Controller)		
Technology (Chief Technology Officer, Website developer, tech support staff)		
Human Resources (Personnel Director)		
Support Staff (Administrative assistants, Office Manager, etc.)		
Other		

WHO DO I NEED ON MY TEAM?

Desired Attitudes/Habits	Education	Skills	Compensation

Of course, with a young company, you don't want to hire more people than absolutely necessary. Since revenues are uncertain, it's better to start conservatively and add staff—whether full-time or part-time employees or contractors—as your business grows and customer demand increases.

As you plan how to grow your business, look at what managerial roles need to be filled and what kinds of people you'd most like to have fill them. You can then create job descriptions and, assuming you've got the money to cover your payroll expenses, begin recruiting.

Some of the key positions you may need to fill:

- **Administrative**
- **Sales/Customer Service**
- **Billing/Bookkeeping**
- **Production**
- **Shipping**
- **Marketing**
- **Technology**

Use the worksheet on the previous two pages to identify the positions you need to fill and the specifics of each job.

3. Examine the use of independent contractors

Most companies use outside providers to perform certain tasks. It's not necessary to handle every function—even relatively critical functions—with people you employ on your own staff.

You can outsource all kinds of responsibilities, including bookkeeping, website design and hosting, payroll management, public relations, marketing, employee training, and even many aspects of production.

To provide these functions, you can use other companies or hire self-employed individuals—independent contractors.

Indeed, it may be that you—or your business—might serve as an outside provider of services or an independent contractor for other companies. This is especially true if you're providing services like those listed above.

Few areas of employment law are murkier than who qualifies as an independent contractor for tax purposes and who doesn't. And few areas of tax law can get a business—or an independent contractor—in more trouble with HMRC. Here's why:

As a business owner, you—naturally—want to reduce your costs as much as possible. When you hire someone to work for you, you can pay them in one of two ways:

- **as an employee:** paying additional payroll, Social Security, and unemployment taxes, (and typically providing benefits); or

- **as an independent contractor:** paying no additional taxes (and typically not providing any benefits).

As an individual working for others, you can work:

- **as an employee:** receiving less money in your pocket due to withholding taxes but also receiving more legal protections and typically more benefits; or

- **as an independent contractor:** often getting more money in your pocket since there are no withholding taxes, but also not receiving benefits and little or no worker protection, and also having to deal with the hassle and paperwork of handing and paying your own taxes quarterly or at the end of the year.

Obviously, many businesses would prefer to treat "employees" as independent contractors and avoid all those pesky taxes and worker protections. Equally obviously, the government wants to make certain that anyone who's really doing the work of an employee gets treated—and protected—as such, and that all payroll and Social Security taxes are paid.

So watch out! HMRC is particularly aggressive in pursuing companies that intentionally—or unintentionally—inappropriately pay workers as independent contractors instead of as employees. HMRC has gone after huge corporations as well as small businesses, and once they find a violation, they're likely to go back through many past years of your taxes.

Making the use of independent contractors even more difficult is that HMRC guidelines aren't crystal clear. There used to be a list of specific rules governing independent contractor status, but HMRC, responding to the legitimate needs of businesses for greater flexibility in hiring independent contractors, made the rules broader. But that means there's more room for misunderstanding.

The main issue HMRC tries to determine is who "controls" the worker. They look at three areas:

- **Behavioural:** does the worker control how they do the work? In other words, HMRC looks at issues such as who controls:

  - **when and where the worker does the work**
  - **what tools or equipment they use**
  - **who determines where they purchase supplies**
  - **what order or sequence of work to follow**

- **Financial:** Does the worker have a significant investment (e.g., own their own tools)? Can they make a profit or loss? Do they make their services available to others and/or work for other businesses?

- **Type of relationship:** How permanent is the relationship? Is there a written contract? Is the worker responsible for their own benefits? Is the work performed a critical and regular part of the business?

Because the rules are somewhat fuzzy, HMRC does provide some protection for businesses that make mistakes in treating employees as independent contractors—as long as those mistakes were made in good faith. They'll look to see whether a business relied on advice of a lawyer or accountant, followed industry practice, treated workers consistently.

As an employer, before using independent contractors, consider the impact on your workers' productivity. Legitimate, self-employed contractors are usually highly-motivated to do a good job; they want to keep you as a client and have you refer others. The opposite happens when a business needs employees—with definite work hours, specific work, and being directly managed by supervisors—but treats them as independent contractors. Such workers are demoralised, less productive, eager to find better employment, and more likely to call HMRC if you're not following the law.

If you plan on using independent contractors, be certain to ask your lawyer (this week) about how to stay well within the law, and check with your accountant (Week Five) about filing all necessary tax forms.

The Government imposes several laws on compensation, treatment, and protection of employees. Among the many regulations your business must follow are the following:

RED TAPE ALERT!

- Safety rules and record keeping
- Minimum wage and child labour laws
- Tax withholdings
- Insurance requirements
- Anti-discrimination laws
- Immigration laws
- Family and medical leave laws
- Employee vs. independent contractor distinctions

4. Understand employment laws and consider your personnel policies

As soon as you decide to hire your first employee, you'll need to understand critical personnel laws. There are many government protections for workers, as well as extra taxes and obligations on you as an employer. Such things as questions you can't ask in an interview, how many hours an employee can work without getting paid overtime, even how long a lunch break must be are all covered under labour laws. You want to avoid running into any trouble just because you inadvertently violated employment laws.

Additionally, you'll need to come up with basic personnel policies: benefits, vacation, holidays, sick days, working hours and so forth. Even in a very small company, a written set of policies helps create a sense of security and fairness for employees.

Developing company policies doesn't mean you need a five-inch thick rule book. You can develop a simple set of policies, listing:

- **Number of vacation days earned each year, and how many of these days can be carried forwarded if not used**
- **Number of sick days each year**

MY PERSONNEL POLICIES

Always check with a lawyer or human resources specialist before finalising your personnel policies, as the law may affect what you may or may not do regarding overtime, work hours, family leave, etc.

Work Hours

Starting time: _____

Ending time: _____

Flex time policies: _____

Overtime policies: _____

Other: _____

Vacation Days

Number of days per year: _____

When do they become available? _____

Increases after years of service? How many? _____

Can unused vacation days be accumulated? How many? How long? _____

What times of year can they be taken? How do they have to notify you? _____

Sick Leave

How many paid sick days off per year? _____

Can they be accumulated? _____

Special circumstances? _____

Personal Leave

Will you allow any paid personal leave time? How much? _____

_____

How much notice do employees have to give for personal leave? _____

Holidays

Which holidays will be time off with pay? _____

_____

Any "floating" holidays? _____

Any other time-off policies, either paid or unpaid, sabbaticals, etc.? _____

_____

Reimbursement Policies?

Which expenses will the company reimburse employees for? (e.g., travel, commute, parking, public transportation):

_____

How will those have to be documented/submitted? _____

_____

MY PERSONNEL POLICIES

Insurance

List the insurance coverage you'll offer and how and whether dependents are covered:

Health Insurance: _____

Dental Insurance: _____

Vision Insurance: _____

Life Insurance: _____

Disability: _____

Other: _____

Retirement Programme

Will you offer a retirement plan? _____

List details: who is covered, when do they vest, what amount employees have to contribute, etc.:

_____

_____

Training/Education

What ongoing training will you offer employees? _____

Will you reimburse/pay for non-company-sponsored education/training programmes/tuition?

_____

Benefits

List any other special perks/benefits offered (e.g., mobile phones, car leased, birthdays off, etc.):

_____

_____

Employees who are Telecommuting/Home Offices

What reimbursements do you offer them? (e.g., phone, Internet connection, mobile phone, office supplies, electricity, furniture allowance, etc.): _____

_____

How do they get reimbursements (submit monthly form or give ongoing amount?): _____

How many days/weeks are they expected to be at the main office? _____

Other: _____

Performance Review

How often will you do performance reviews? _____

On what basis will performance be judged? _____

Who will participate in reviewing employees? _____

Other: _____

- **Number of personal leave days, and whether these can be taken as partial days**
- **Paid holidays**
- **Working hours**

In a very small company—with very motivated staff—you may be able to keep these issues flexible (as long as you follow the law, of course).

As you develop your company policies, be clear, allow flexibility when you can, and above all, be fair. Treating people fairly does not necessarily mean treating people equally: a salesperson may need a paid mobile phone; a stockroom clerk may not. An employee with a terminally-ill relative may need more flexible work schedules than others. Part of your job as an employer is to constantly examine your own actions for bias. Apply the same standards—not the same rules—to all.

Sometimes you can't be flexible—rules have to be followed. This is particularly true when company policy is dictated by law. When you have to follow inflexible rules, let employees know why. Is it for safety, to obey laws, or to meet certain standards? Help people understand why a rule isn't silly.

Use the worksheet on the previous two pages to establish the main policies your business will follow in dealing with employees.

Finding and hiring good people

Your business is only as good as the people who work for it. No matter how good your product, how necessary your service, how innovative your technology, it's the people in your company that will ultimately determine your success. That's why it's important to find the right people, then train, nurture and reward them.

When you have an immediate need for help, you might be tempted to hire anyone you can get, but it's often better to leave a position unfilled until you can find a person you consider capable and trustworthy.

Here's something to keep in mind right from the star: Hire for attitude, train for skills. You want people on your team with good work habits, a positive attitude, and an ability to get along with others. In most cases, you can teach a smart and willing person a particular skill (such as how to use a software program or operate a piece of machinery). It's much more challenging—and a lot more work—to instill the right attitude in the wrong person.

Keeping it simple

Nordstrom, the upscale department store, became famous for their outstanding customer service. How does Nordstrom instill such dedication and loyalty in its employees? One factor may be its personnel policies. The Nordstrom personnel manual contains only one sentence: "Use good judgement in all situations."

RECRUITING EMPLOYEES

What recruitment efforts will you use to find employees?
What ongoing training will you offer employees?
What features of your company and/or specific job do you want to mention in your ads?
What unusual or particularly appealing aspects of your company and/or specific job can you describe that would make you stand out from others?
Other aspects to mention in ads or interviews:

List specific places you could advertise/look for employees:

Newspapers: _____

Online career/hiring sites: _____

Schools/Colleges/Universities: _____

Career fairs: _____

Trade organisations: _____

Other organisations: _____

Bulletin boards: _____

Unemployment offices: _____

Other media: _____

Former employees: _____

Other referral sources: _____

Competitors: _____

Others: _____

It's often difficult to find enough qualified applicants for a job. Extend your job-hunting efforts beyond the usual means of a newspaper classified ad. Use your network with others, especially other entrepreneurs, and ask for referrals of any prospective job applicants.

Here are other ways to increase the quality of job applicants:

- **Create an ongoing recruitment campaign:** Develop a network of referral sources, and remind everyone in your company to be on the look-out for great employees.

QUESTIONS TO ASK   POTENTIAL EMPLOYEES

Don't wait until a job applicant is sitting in the waiting room before figuring out what to ask. Take time well before the first interview and make a list of things you'd like to know about someone before you hire them, such as whether they have the right experience, skills, education, etc. Ask specific questions in those areas, "What were your exact responsibilities?" "What computer programs did you use regularly?" And so on. Find out, also, what they liked and didn't like about their previous jobs and what they hope for in their new position. That gives you a better sense of whether they are a good fit for your job and your company.

During interviews, don't do all the talking! It's appropriate to explain the job, and in many cases, to try and 'sell' the job to the candidate, but most of the time the candidate should be talking, not you. You may want to have others also interview the applicant, especially the prospect's direct manager, and possibly co-workers and even people who will work for him or her.

In addition to direct work related questions, it's important to ask questions that give you a sense of the applicant as a person and their attitudes toward responsibility, working in a team, how flexible they are when faced with change or uncertainty, etc. But be careful! Some questions are illegal to ask. You can't, for instance, ask whether a candidate is planning on having a child, their marital status, religion, age (in many cases). But it's perfectly legal to ask about hobbies, interests, and long-term goals.

And never, never discriminate on the basis of race, gender, age, national origin, etc. It's not just illegal—you'll eliminate some terrific potential employees.

- **Be creative in your ads:** When you place a "help-wanted ad," create as much attention and interest as possible. Express the "personality" of your company in your ads.

- **Hire the unusual:** Increase your applicant pool by expanding your vision of a typical employee. Does your industry usually hire young people? Try recruiting retirees. How about looking for employees with disabilities? Or from different ethnic groups? Sometimes the best employees don't look like the ones you already have.

- **Be in the game on salary and benefits:** As a new company, you may not be able to pay more than big companies or give as many benefits, but you better be fairly competitive. You can't be so far apart that any applicant would feel like a fool for accepting your job.

- **Offer creative 'perks:'** We allow employees to bring their dogs to work; I give employees their birthday as a paid holiday. One of the best perks is flexibility. An applicant may want to start work at 10 am to avoid rush hour and stay later, or come to work earlier and leave at 3:30 pm to be home with the kids after school. Of course, this isn't always possible, but flexibility is a highly desired job benefit.

- **Act fast:** If you see someone you really like, be prepared to decide and make an offer. But don't ever hire out of desperation; it's better to keep a job open than be stuck with the wrong person.

- **Get a reputation as a great place to work:** Sure, all applicants look at tangible benefits. But in the long run, what encourages current employees to recruit others, reduces turnover, and attracts the best new applicants, is building a business where people feel good about going to work—a company with integrity, respect for all, and where people also have fun. Do that, and you'll have them lining up at your door.

Use the worksheet on page 113 to identify places to seek employees.

Compensation

To attract good employees, you have to offer salaries and benefits that are competitive with similar businesses in your area. Most employees' main financial concern is the salary or wage offered, but they will also decide to accept a job based on the total "package," including:

- **Base salary/wage**

RED TAPE ALERT! Discrimination. It's not good business. It's not good behaviour. And it's against the law. In virtually all situations, it is illegal to discriminate against employees because of race, religion, sex, or national origin. In many situations, it's illegal to discriminate on the basis of age, physical disability, or sexual orientation. You may not discriminate in hiring, promotion, pay, or treatment. Moreover, it is your responsibility as an employer to create an environment that is not hostile to any individual or group based on such factors. You must also make "reasonable accommodation" to employees' religious observance needs, such as allowing them time off on their sabbaths or holy days or wearing articles of religious attire (unless there is a significant safety concern).

- **Bonuses, based either on individual performance, group or company performance, or guaranteed bonus**
- **Overtime, which may be set by law**
- **Signing bonus, as an incentive in a very tight job market**
- **Commissions, given on sales made**
- **Profit sharing, a portion of the overall company profits**
- **Stock options or stock purchase plans, giving the employee a discounted means to purchase a direct financial stake in the company.**

To determine the "going rate" for compensation packages in your industry and region, consult human resource/personnel specialists and other businesspeople. In tight labour markets, you're obviously going to have to offer higher salaries and benefits.

Benefits

In addition to direct cash payments and/or stock, most jobs offer a range of other benefits. Typically, these include paid vacation, sick leave, health insurance, and retirement benefits. Large companies may offer a wider range of benefits than smaller or newer companies, but this isn't always the case, and good employees expect a decent package of basic benefits.

Benefits can be powerful motivators for employees. But devising a benefits package is not necessarily easy. Besides the cost of benefits (especially health insurance) there are questions of fairness, such as whether employees' children should be covered. If so, should childless employees receive an equal total pound benefit package?

Sometimes small perks are appreciated, such as free drinks, snacks, or other food. "Creative" perks often appeal to certain employees.

The "Personnel Policies" worksheet on pages 110–111 includes space to list insurance and other benefits you want to offer employees.

Training

Just as you have to continually improve your own skills, you want to continually improve the capabilities of your employees. The best companies make a strong commitment to ongoing training and education.

Often the easiest way to provide training, especially for a small company, is to pay for employees to attend outside seminars or classes. These are offered by a wide range of providers. As your company grows, you may want to develop some in-house training programmes or bring in seminar leaders or speakers.

Don't just provide training for specific skills. While these may be necessary, it's also beneficial to educate employees in broader areas, such as overall business strategy, industry trends, etc. The smarter, more knowledgeable an employee, the more he or she can contribute to your success.

5. Appraise your management style

When you run a small company, you can't afford to waste resources, yet many business owners often squander one of their most valuable assets: their employees. I'm always surprised when I encounter an employer who views having employees as a necessary evil to be endured rather than a resource to be developed. If you waste the intelligence, energy, or skills of employees, it's like throwing money out the window.

Your attitude towards the people you hire goes a long way in determining their attitude about the job they do. The surest way to get the most from employees is to treat each with respect. No matter what kind of work a person does, they like to have a sense that their opinion and input counts. When you allow your employees to think about how to solve problems, not just carry out specific tasks, you can unleash an amazing amount of creativity and energy.

But having employees is also a challenge. In addition to dealing with all the laws, paperwork, and policies, you've got to deal with employees as people—each with a distinct personality. That means some of your time is going to be diverted from specific tasks to personality issues—how people get along, communicate, and solve problems. You can view this as a distraction from your "real" work or you can recognise that this is part of the job of being a boss.

Being a boss is tough. It's one of the most demanding challenges of running a company. You have to inspire, lead, motivate, discipline, and reward. Some of the most important leadership skills include:

- **Communicating goals:** Let people know why they are doing something, not just how to do it; employees are far more motivated when they understand the purpose of a task.

- **Setting standards:** You are responsible for establishing—and demonstrating—the standards you expect others to maintain.

- **Being fair:** Make sure your standards are reasonable and fair, and that goals are actually reachable.

- **Listening:** Learn to talk *with* and not just talk *to* your employees; enlist their suggestions and set goals together.

- **Making decisions:** The buck has to stop somewhere; employees look to their leaders to make choices and stick with them.

Rewarding and acknowledging

Everyone wants acknowledgement for a job well done. Few things are more dispiriting than to excel at a task and then have your hard work ignored. Moreover, it's just human nature to try harder to please those who appreciate us than those who ignore us.

Give credit to all employees who do their job well, with particular rewards for those who perform exceptionally. Give praise quickly and publicly. If you need to discipline an employee, do that privately. Find fun or creative ways to congratulate people. But often, just a public "thank you" or a round of applause shows that you've noticed their contribution. Take time to celebrate successes, especially with everyone in the company. It's a morale booster.

So what kind of boss will you be? Will you have the skills to lead your company rather than micro-manage your employees? Can you create an

MY LEADERSHIP SKILLS

Rate yourself in each area below as either: excellent, good, fair, or needs to improve.

Skill	Excellent	Good	Fair	Needs Work
Decision making				
Communicating goals				
Setting standards				
Listening				
Consistently being fair				
Patience				
Creating a learning atmosphere				
Training others				
Motivating others to do their best				
Constructively communicating problems/disagreements				
Acknowledging and rewarding the contributions of others				
Other leadership skills:				

List things you'll do to improve your leadership and management skills (classes, training, books, etc.):

environment that encourages employees to do their best? The Leadership Skills Assessment worksheet on on the previous page lets you evaluate your own experiences and abilities as a leader.

Pay attention to choosing, training, developing, and rewarding the people on your team because they are your most important resource. One of the best ways to motivate employees is to make your company an organisation they're proud to work for. Everyone, including your employees, wants a sense of pride and purpose in what they do.

week 4

TAKE CARE OF OPERATIONS

Main accomplishments:

- ✓ Find and secure a location
- ✓ Design your work and production space
- ✓ Research and purchase equipment
- ✓ Research and purchase technology
- ✓ Design procedures for handling administrative tasks
- ✓ Deal with insurance

Make appointments with:

- ✓ Estate agent
- ✓ Suppliers
- ✓ Insurance agent

take care o

operations

WHERE WILL YOU WORK, MAKE, OR SELL YOUR PRODUCTS? What kind of equipment do you need? How will you keep track of paperwork? Even something as basic as a desk and a chair can turn your business into a reality, but which desk? Which chair?

During this week, you'll deal with issues such as choosing a place to work, selecting furniture and equipment, purchasing inventory, and handling the day-to-day mundane aspects required to turn your vision into an operational business.

How you handle the day-to-day operations and administration of your company directly affects your success. While these details may seem mundane, in fact, they may make all the difference in whether you are profitable, have sufficient cash flow to pay your bills, or stay out of trouble with authorities. The wrong location can doom a retail business; a poor manufacturing process can result in higher costs, lower quality, or too much waste. These issues are so important you may want to develop a detailed Operations Plan or manual to outline your processes in greater detail.

ACCOMPLISHMENT #1:
Find and secure a location

How important is location to the success of your business? If you have a business serving a particular neighbourhood or community, you need to be physically located in or near that area. If you're in retail, the choice of location is absolutely critical and may determine whether you have enough customers to stay in business. A factor as seemingly insignificant as which side of a particular street you're on can dramatically affect the amount of customer traffic you'll receive.

If you're a manufacturer, you'll need access to raw materials, a shipping system (whether that's lorries, air, ships, or rail), and a good labour force, but location may otherwise not be that important.

And then there are lots of companies that provide services from a distance (thanks in large part to recent technologies such as the Internet) so business needs don't direct their choice of location at all.

Even if the site of your business doesn't seem critical, the choice of your facilities and neighbourhood has an impact on how you and your employees feel about coming to work. A pleasant building, in a safe neighbourhood, with nearby parking and friendly neighbours can make work more enjoyable. It can even help in recruiting employees.

Many entrepreneurs know exactly where they want to work—at home! Working at home can be a great advantage but it also presents some challenges especially if you have children or spouses there. Planning your home office—its space, storage, and policies—helps you make the most of this arrangement.

Some people run their businesses almost entirely from their vehicles—cars, lorries, vans. If you work from a vehicle, plan that "office," too.

In this section, the tasks of finding and securing your location depends on what kind of space you're planning for your business, either:

- **rented space**
- **home office**
- **office in a vehicle**

Go to the section appropriate for your business to see the tasks associated with your needs.

OPTION 1:

Rent space

Tasks:

☐ 1. **Decide on the necessary attributes of your location**

☐ 2. **Meet with an estate agent**

☐ 3. **Compare properties**

☐ 4. **Consider whether you need more than one location**

1. Decide on the necessary attributes of your location

Before you begin to search for rented space, prioritise your needs. Generally, this depends on what kind of business you're in—retail, manufacturing, service, or another type of industry—and your specific business activities. For instance, as a publisher, my company deals with heavy boxes of books daily. So when we looked for new facilities, even for our administrative offices, we wanted to find space on the ground floor or with lift access, so we didn't have to carry those heavy boxes up flights of stairs.

Don't forget less-tangible issues, especially ones important to the quality of life for you and your employees. After all, you aren't starting your own business to hate the place you go to work! In my case, I wanted offices where I could still walk to work from home, and where employees could bring their dogs. Those issues certainly narrowed our search further.

Of course, you need to figure out about how much space you need and what your budget can handle. You may want to start small—with a short-term lease—until you are somewhat well-established.

As you ponder the necessary attributes of your space, consider your needs depending on the use of your facilities:

Office/Administrative: Virtually all businesses need at least some office space. Many businesses only need office space—professional, sales, or administrative offices. On the other hand, if the main purpose of your

THINGS TO CONSIDER WHEN RENTING SPACE

✓	Questions and terms to negotiate in lease	Notes
	Cost of rent: Does my rent require me also to pay the taxes, insurance, or even a percent of my income? Am I required to pay a portion of rent on "common areas"?	
	Length of lease and subletting: Can I get an option to renew? At what rent? Can I sublet some or all of the space?	
	Layout: Does the layout of the space suit my work style or production needs? Is there lots of wasted space I pay for?	
	Leasehold improvements/remodeling: Who is responsible for improving the facility — me or the landlord? Am I responsible for returning the facility back to its original condition when I move?	
	Utilities: What utilities are included in the rent? Are adequate utilities available—electricity, water, heat?	
	Janitorial/Maintenance: Who is responsible for cleaning and repairs? Who is responsible for waste disposal?	
	Zoning laws and other use restrictions: Are there any limits on how I may make use of the premises?	
	Permits/Planning departments: What kind of permits will I need to operate my business or remodel? What are the costs and time involved?	
	Storage: Is there adequate space for storing supplies, raw materials, inventory? Is it easily accessible?	
	Furniture/Equipment: Does the space come with any furniture, equipment, or fixtures? If so, are those included in the rent?	
	Safety/Security: Is the location safe for employees, customers, and my equipment and inventory?	
	Expansion: Is there sufficient space for me to grow? How soon will my needs exceed this space?	
	Environmental: What environmental limitations or concerns apply to this space? Is noise a factor — either noise I produce or noise from outside?	
	Insurance: What insurance does the owner have? What insurance must I provide? Will I have any difficulty getting adequate insurance for this location?	
	Access/Parking: Is the site easily accessible for customers, employees, shipments? Are there adequate parking spaces provided? Is it near public transportation?	
✓	**Office space considerations**	Notes
	Appearance: Will I be meeting clients or customers at the office and need to make a positive impression? Does the office have a waiting area?	

THINGS TO CONSIDER WHEN RENTING SPACE

✓	Office space considerations (continued)	Notes
	Privacy: Does the office have sufficient privacy for my business needs?	
	Meeting space/conference rooms: Do I have sufficient access to conference rooms or other meeting space?	
	Mail shipping and receiving: Can I receive mail or shipments? Is it secure? What time does it arrive?	
	Coffee/kitchen/eating areas: Is there access to any coffee, food preparation or eating areas? Is water convenient?	
	Lighting: Does the space have adequate lighting to avoid eye strain and fatigue for me and employees?	
	Wiring/data lines: Is the space already wired for high-speed Internet access? If not, will it be difficult or expensive to install wiring?	
✓	Retail space considerations	Notes
	History of others in the space: How have other retail or restaurant businesses fared at this location?	
	Fellow tenants/neighbours: Are the retail neighbours compatible, with similar market demographics?	
	Quality of the space itself: Does it feel welcoming and make it easy to show off my merchandise?	
	Limitations on space, additional fees: Are there any limits on my hours of operation, or requirements to pay additional fees or participate in certain promotions (common in malls or business improvement districts)?	
✓	Manufacturing space considerations	Notes
	Docks/shipping facilities: Can I receive/ship my expected materials/inventory? Does the location incur additional shipping fees?	
	Utilities: Are there adequate utilities for my production needs — water, electricity, natural gas, etc.	
	Waste disposal: Is there adequate access and cost for waste disposal, including any hazardous materials resulting from my production process?	
	Proximity to suppliers and distributors: How long will it take to replenish materials, to send my product to distributors and customers? Costs?	
✓	Other lease provisions?	Notes
	What other fees, duties, or limitations are part of the lease agreement?	

business is retail or manufacturing, your "office" may only be a small portion of your total site.

Since you are just starting out, and if your company has just one or two staff people, one approach to office space may be to rent an "Executive Suite" office or to find space to sublet from another company. This gets you up-and-running much faster, since it may be set up with furniture, Internet access, conference room, and the use of office equipment (copiers, printers, fax machine). It may also give you the flexibility of a short-term or month-to-month lease.

Retail: Location, location, location. One of the most important considerations for a retail business is the choice of location. Do you want to be in a mall? On a popular pedestrian street? In a particular neighbourhood?

If your business is easily seen by passers-by (such as in a mall or well-trafficked street) you can save considerably on marketing and advertising costs. Of course, these locations typically charge higher rent. However, paying higher rent to get a more visible and accessible space may be well worth it.

Besides being seen by customers, they have to be able to get to your store easily. If customers have easy access—either walking, driving, or taking public transportation—you have a competitive advantage over businesses that are hard to reach or find.

Manufacturing/Production: What do you make? Toys? Computer peripherals? Packaged organic vegetables? Obviously, the nature of your product dictates the kind of facilities you need.

Your production facilities can have a direct impact on your profitability. Is it set up to save on energy use and costs? Can you lay out your production processes efficiently? Are you near your customers or shipping facilities? How much does it cost to have waste removed? Understand all costs and benefits as you choose your space.

Also consider whether you need your own facilities or whether there are contract manufacturing facilities available. Some industries have contract manufacturing/production facilities (such as contract kitchens) that give you the flexibility to start up without investing large sums of capital.

Warehouse/Storage: Some facilities are used primarily for storage. In these situations, you have many of the same concerns as manufacturing:

shipping, docks, utilities, safety, access, security, and proximity to distributors. Be particularly cautious of environmental considerations that may affect the products/materials you are storing.

Use the worksheet on pages 132–133 for a more detailed checklist of issues related to renting space. It includes items of general concern if you are renting space, and items specific to the type of space you are renting.

2. Meet with an estate agent

Once you know what you need, you can start shopping for space.

The first thing to do is to start driving—or walking—around the area that interests you. You might want to drive around a few different areas before settling in on your first choice. You're likely to find some "For Rent" signs if there are lots of properties available.

However, commercial properties are harder to find than residential. They're not as likely to be listed in the newspaper or online, and often, there's not even a "For Rent" sign in available commercial property windows. There isn't a "Multiple Listing Service" as there is for home sales.

As a result, you're probably going to want to work with a commercial estate agent, especially if you need a lot of space.

You'll have to be persistent. It's often difficult to get fast action from agents or landlords if you only need a small amount of space. So you have to stay on top of the process.

Find an estate agent who specialises in either the location that interests you or your type of business. Ask other entrepreneurs if they have any agents to recommend.

Remember, most commercial estate agents represent landlords and specific properties, so you may end up working with different agents for different properties. Make sure you have someone who's looking out for your interests review any leases or contracts you sign.

3. Compare properties

Once you start looking for space, you'll need to know common commercial estate rental practices and terms.

LOCATION/SPACE COMPARISON CHART

	Location One	Location Two	Location Three
Address/Contact info			
Total sq. feet			
Rent (per sq.ft., total)			
Length of lease (option to renew, at what rent?)			
What's included? (utilities, janitor, data lines?)			
What am I responsible for? (utilities, janitor, data lines?)			
Legal issues (permits, zoning, etc.)			
Parking, access, and safety issues			
Insurance issues			
Advantages			
Disadvantages			
Other			

Typically, you'll be quoted rental prices on a "per square foot" or "sf" basis. (If you're subletting or renting executive office space, you might be quoted a flat rate). In most of the UK, the square foot price is given on an annualised basis (e.g., £12 a square foot).

Before you make your first call, familiarise yourself with terms brokers and landlords toss around. *Beware!* Definitions vary from landlord to landlord, so have them make clear what is included.

The vast majority of agreements will exclude any extras such as utilities, maintenance and possibly insurance. They will add a service charge and here it is vital to find out what that includes. It can mean anything from running water to a full receptionist service in a shared premises, and ideally the cost will reflect this.

Whether you are using your space for retail (a shop), administrative (office), manufacturing (a plant), or storage purposes (a warehouse), you face many of the same considerations. The chart at right and the checklist on pages 132–133 can help you as you shop. You may also want to use the checklist as a basis for negotiating terms with your landlord.

That brings us to the question of how long a lease to ask for. This depends on the stability and stage of your business, the quality and price of the space, your future plans, and your comfort level with taking on a long-term obligation. As a new business, you may be better off with a short-term lease, even if rents go up in the future, or you have to move. If you take a long-term lease, make certain you can sublet it.

And remember, before you sign any contract, including a lease, go over it with your solicitor first.

4. Consider whether you need more than one location

In some instances, you may need more than one location for your business. If you are in manufacturing, you may find it less expensive or necessary to have your manufacturing facilities in one city and your administrative or sales offices elsewhere. An apparel manufacturer may want a sales office in Edinburgh, for example, while the actual production occurs in Aberdeen.

In most types of business, technology has made it relatively simple to have some workers who are "remotely located," often far away from the main office. This may be a good option if you want to hire individuals with certain skills who are located far from your main place of business.

Be warned, however: having more than one site presents a number of legal and logistical issues, in addition to the challenge of getting more than one business location up-and-running. After all, it's hard enough to start a business in one place; why give yourself the added burden of operating in more than one location unless you have a pressing need?

You are particularly going to run into legal and tax issues if you have workers (even non-employees) in more than one state. Having a "presence" in another state may trigger your obligation to collect sales tax on purchases in that state (see Week Three). You may also have to deal with that state's payroll, business, and income taxes. Each state may have different insurance regulations, and if you are offering health insurance, you may need to get different providers for each state.

WHAT WOULD RHONDA DO?

SERVING ANOTHER LOCATION

Do you want to make sales in another city, but you don't have the money to open and staff a second store or office? One approach I'd use is to get a "remote location number" from the phone company. With a remote location number, you get a local phone number in your target city and a listing in that city's local phone directory. However, all calls are immediately forwarded to your regular phone number. Voila! You can serve another community even though you don't have a store or office or even a phone instrument there. You pay a small monthly fee plus toll calls from the target city to your local phone, if any. This is also a good idea if you're moving; you can keep your former phone number, along with your customers, in your former city.

OPTION 2:
Set up a home office

Tasks:

☐ 1. **Find the space to work**

☐ 2. **Figure out your phone, fax, and Internet connections**

☐ 3. **Plan how to meet with customers**

☐ 4. **Decide whether you need a separate business address**

☐ 5. **Understand home-based office tax deductions**

☐ 6. **Deal with the kids and pets**

For many years, I ran my business from my home. I enjoyed working from home, and I never had more than what I jokingly called my "one room commute." When I finally decided to lease office space, I left home with some regret. Running a business from home has many advantages, but it has its challenges as well. The key is to set up a home office right.

1. Find the space to work

A home office can take many forms. It might simply be one end of your dining room table. It could be the guest room, as long as no guests come to visit. You might claim a section of your garage, and even build in walls and install a window, shelves, heating, and air conditioning.

If you're serious about your business, you need good work space. You don't necessarily need a separate room, but find a space without too many distractions. Once you've chosen the physical space for your office, consider what will go in it:

■ **A desk or work table.** At the very minimum, you should have a desk or table used only for work. Having to clear your stuff off the dining room table every night quickly gets old. Make certain it's the right height for what you're doing.

■ **A good chair.** Get out of that folding chair and buy yourself something comfortable enough to sit in for hours. Your shoulders and back will thank you.

■ **Good lighting.** Most homes don't have sufficient lighting to work all day, so in addition to overhead and indirect lighting, get a desk light. Don't put your computer monitor directly in front of a window (you'll squint all day), and watch for glare from other windows.

■ **Heaters or air conditioners.** The temperature in your office is more than just a matter of personal comfort (which is very important). If you have equipment in your office, you need a stable temperature. I ruined a computer hard drive because my office was in a room that got very cold at night and condensation formed on the drive.

■ **Storage.** When you run a business from home, you accumulate stuff—a lot of stuff! You need someplace to put it. Purchase an office-type storage cabinet or put shelves up in a closet. Put stuff you need to use frequently within easy reach. Trust me, you'll underestimate the amount of storage space you need.

■ **Electricity.** Surge protector strips have the benefit of increasing the number of your electrical outlets, but be careful not to overload circuits. Buy the kind of surge protectors that can handle 'transformers'—those big electrical plugs on many technology devices.

2. Figure out your phone, fax, and Internet connections

I'm a big believer in a separate business phone line if you're doing business from your home on an ongoing basis. Once your toddler answers a call from your most important client, you'll see the necessity of a separate line for incoming business calls. If you want to be listed in the Yellow Pages or "business" section of the phone book, many local phone companies require you to have a "business" line. An extra phone line for business also enables you to have a business message on that line and a family message on your other line.

If you receive a high volume of faxes or use a dial-up Internet connection, get a separate data line as well.

Above all, if you're going to be working from your home full-time, get a high-speed Internet connection, if you haven't already – and remember if you're planning to use your existing connection you might not get the fast service you need as a business if it breaks down. Once you get used to fast service and being permanently connected to the Internet, it makes email communication and finding information much easier. You can get high-speed connections via DSL (typically from your phone company) or through a cable modem (typically from your cable television provider). If neither service is available in your area, a third option is a satellite system, though this can be a bit more costly and, as of this writing, less reliable.

If you're going to have more than one person using your Internet connection at a time, or use your connection in more than one room, purchase an Internet "router." These little boxes allow multiple computers to share the same Internet connection. Some will even allow your computers to connect to them "wirelessly," so you don't need to string networking cables all over your house (you'll need to install "wireless cards" in each of your computers, however).

3. Plan how to meet with customers

If you work out of your home, one of the biggest challenges is often figuring out where and when to meet with customers. If you only meet customers at their place of business, at trade shows, or over the Internet, no problem! But if customers are going to come to you, how will you arrange your space so you look professional?

If you're going to be meeting with others regularly, ideally, you want to set up your work space separately from your family surroundings. If possible, have a separate entrance or at least a path to your office that doesn't go through a messy playroom or kitchen. If you're meeting clients infrequently, or on a regular schedule, you may be able to use your own living or dining room as a meeting space. Just make sure the rest of the family, if any, know to stay away!

What if you don't want customers in your home but need to meet them somewhere other than their offices? Look for other, "neutral" locations, such as a lunch meeting in a restaurant. If you have an ongoing need, find another company that will allow you to "sublet" or "rent" a meeting space or conference room on an hourly basis (such as a small law firm). "Executive suite" services—short-term office rentals—often offer hourly rentals as well.

4. Decide whether you need a separate business address

When you work from home, you face a dilemma: what address should you give out?

If you use only your home address, are you comfortable putting it on business cards and marketing brochures that you hand to strangers, or put on a website where the world can see it? If you don't put any address on these marketing materials, you might seem less than professional.

One alternative is to get a Post Office box from the Post Office. The problem, however, is that then your business address is only a post office box—or "P.O. Box"—number. That may make your business seem somewhat insubstantial. Moreover, the UK Post Office usually refuses to accept deliveries from private delivery services such as FedEx or UPS.

5. Understand home-based office tax deductions

When you work from home, one murky area you'll need to deal with is which business expenses are deductible and which aren't. If you buy a new work table that you use for both your office and for the kids' homework projects, is that deductible? If you add a space heater to your office in the garage, can you deduct the extra utility expenses? What if you let your kids use your office supplies?

Tax deductions for home offices are daunting and confusing. If you're setting up a home office, you should add these questions to the list when you meet with an accountant (Week Five).

Most normal business expenses that you'd have whether or not you were working from home—postage, office supplies, advertising, wages—are treated the same way as any other business. You can deduct those expenses as part of your regular deductions for the cost of doing business.

Some deductions become more problematic, especially when the expense is—or could be—used for both business and personal purposes, such as telephones, Internet connections, equipment.

You also have an additional tax savings option on your home office if you qualify, and if you choose to take it—the home office deduction. The home office deduction allows you to deduct a portion of your rent or mortgage based on the percent of your home or partment used exclusively for business. That can be a nice extra tax deduction for you.

However, there are many considerations before you take the home office deduction. Also, there are tax implications if you later sell your home. So you certainly want to discuss the home office deduction—and whether you should take it or skip it—with your accountant or tax advisor. Use the guide "Questions to Ask: On Home Office Deductions" to get your conversation started.

QUESTIONS TO ASK   ON HOME OFFICE DEDUCTIONS

✓ What percentage of my rent or mortgage can I deduct?

✓ Can I deduct costs of remodeling? Rewiring?

✓ Can I deduct these expenses the first year, or do I have to capitalise them over a number of years?

✓ Is it wise for me to take the home office deduction?

✓ What are the tax implications if I later sell my home?

✓ What percentage of my phone or Internet connection costs can I deduct?

✓ What percentage of my utilities or other expenses can I deduct?

✓ What furniture and equipment expenses are deductible? Office supplies?

✓ What transportation expenses can I deduct for getting from my office to customers?

✓ Can I deduct expenses for artwork, décor, stereos, or other amenities in my home office?

✓ What other business expenses can I deduct?

Also remember whatever you signed when you moved into your home. Did your landlord or mortgage company stipulate that you wouldn't carry out a business from your home? If so, tell them your plans – as long as you're not going to carry stocks of toxic substances or get loads of visitors they'll probably be fine with it as long as you make the first move to keep them informed. Ditto your home insurance – you probably signed up to 'domestic use only'. Check that you don't invalidate your insurance by working from home, and make sure any equipment you use for work only (like your computer) is covered.

6. Plan ways to separate work life from home life

One of the most difficult tasks for people who work from home is establishing a clear distinction between work and home. If you're not disciplined, you may find yourself distracted by non-business matters. One friend said her house was never cleaner than when she worked from home, since she did housework to avoid taking care of business.

On the other hand, many people who work from home find they never leave "work." They end up working day and night, much to the annoyance of family and friends.

Separating your work life from home life can be especially difficult when you live with others: a spouse, children, or guests who come to visit. Friends and relatives often view home-based entrepreneurs as people who are always available. They don't understand why, in the middle of a work day, you can't run an errand, go to a movie, or pick up kids from school.

The best way to deal with working at home is to be as professional as possible during the time you set aside for business, but allow yourself some of the flexibility you want from working out of your home.

Establish work hours: One of the best ways to protect your valuable personal time yet still have enough time to conduct business is by establishing set work hours.

Structure your week and your workday. Set a work routine that makes you, your family, and others more conscious of your business life. That doesn't mean you have to work from 8 am to 6 pm; just establish real working hours.

For instance, you can tell others (and yourself) something like: "I start work right after I take the kids to school; take a half-hour housecleaning break around 10:30; a quick lunch around 1 pm; go to the post office, run errands, and drop kids off at classes or football from 4 to 6 pm. Then, if I have to, I catch up on paperwork after 9 pm. On Tuesdays and Thursdays, I leave work early to go to exercise class."

Make sure that you, your clients, employees, friends, and family know what your work hours are, when and why you can be interrupted, when you'll take days off, and when your busiest time of the day, week, or year is (so they can leave you alone!).

But also make certain you know when your "free" time is and when your workday is over. It's only fair to others—and yourself—that you "leave" the office after hours and go "home."

Be clear with guests about your spare time: Whether your office is in the guest room or the next town, having guests can be a strain on any home-based entrepreneur. Often, guests don't understand how self-employed people structure their workdays or work weeks.

Allow yourself some time to spend with visitors, but be clear about when you'll be with them and the limits on your availability.

Let prospective guests know in advance how much time you'll be able to spend with them, so they'll understand the situation before they arrive. Put this in the most positive light: "I'm delighted I've been able to cancel my meetings for Thursday afternoon to spend with you. Until then, I'm sure you'll enjoy exploring the city on your own." If you need, make up a list of sights or keep brochures on hand so visitors can find ways to entertain themselves.

Of course, even the best-laid plans may fly out the window when the in-laws arrive!

7. Deal with kids and pets

Many parents find the greatest appeal of a home office is being at home for their children. However, many former work-from-home parents have found, after a year or so of working with crying or demanding children, an office away from home becomes a vital expense.

Make child care arrangements: Be realistic about the demands that kids place on you. It's not realistic to expect to get work done with kids coming in and out, wanting to be driven places, needing a snack, or demanding that you help settle an argument.

Don't imagine, either, that you can just hand your kids off to a friend or neighbour; tomorrow the neighbours' kids may be in your backyard.

Realistically, you may need to make child care arrangements, depending on your childrens' ages and the nature of your work. Some businesses are more flexible in terms of deadlines, hours, or phone calls. Others are truly difficult to run when you have a needy two-year-old or teenager.

As a work-at-home parent, you have some added flexibility in child care arrangements that typical office workers don't. If you have school-aged children, you may be able to schedule your work hours from 9:00 am to 3:00 pm, then spend time with the kids, and return to work at 8:00 pm, when they've gone to bed. You may be able to share child care responsibilities with a spouse—caring for them during the day, and retreating to your home office at 5:00 pm when your spouse gets home from work.

Whatever your arrangement, develop a structured routine for your kids that keeps them busy (and out of your hair) for a set period of time each week so you can get work done. Since you'll naturally want to spend time with your children, set aside specific times. Tell your older children when you'll be available to run errands, make meals, or entertain them.

Pets: If you work at home, a pet is a great companion. A dog or cat makes working at home less lonely. But as someone who had a dog in my own home office for years, I can offer some important tips to making the most of a canine colleague.

- **Barking:** Just as you can't have a screaming child in the background, you can't have a barking dog—at least not too often. If your dog barks uncontrollably, put them in another room.

MOBILE OFFICE PLAN

What will I be using my mobile office to do: (check those that apply)

Make Phone calls	Write up orders	Use Computer
Open mail	Carry passengers	Store samples/literature
Store supplies	Haul equipment	Other hauling
Other issues:		

Other Issues: (check those that apply)

✓	Issue	My Solution
	Cell Phone	
	Storage	
	Writing surface	
	Office supplies	
	Climate control	
	Security	
	Safety	
	Insurance	
	Computer use	
	Internet connection	
	Parking	
	Other issues:	

- **Walking:** Dog walking is an excellent way to meet new people, some of whom might be great networking contacts. I got my very first client walking my late dog, Teddy. A grey terrier mix, Teddy introduced himself to a King Charles Spaniel whose owner happened to need a business plan. Voila! My consulting service was launched.

- **Responsibilities:** If you work alone, (and have a sense of humour) give you dog a "title" in the company. I made Teddy my marketing director since over the years I met many additional clients while walking him.

OPTION 3:
Set up an "office" in your vehicle

Many people run their businesses not from an office or from home, but from a car, van, or truck. In some industries and lines of work—contractors, sales representatives, real estate agents, landscape designers, to name a few—an efficient and workable mobile office is a necessity.

Since many people do not think of their vehicle as an "office," they don't organise the space appropriately. As a result, their "workplace" becomes unworkable, with important notes shoved in the glove compartment or valuable equipment moving around loose in the back of the truck.

If you know you're going to be using your vehicle for business, develop a mobile office plan. There are many commercially available products to outfit cars and trucks for specific purposes, including most kinds of contractors or trades. There are even "desks" for your front seat.

Since your vehicle is your office, you'll also want to assure its contents are safe. You probably don't want to store the only copy of valuable documents or records in your vehicle. Where will you keep those instead? Consider where you will park your vehicle overnight; you want to make sure it's safe and secure.

When you get insurance, make certain your policy covers not only the vehicle itself but also your "office" contents or equipment, especially if you regularly carry expensive tools or equipment. And, of course, talk to your accountant or tax advisor about deductions for your mobile office.

Use the worksheet on the previous page to assist you in planning your "office" in your vehicle.

ACCOMPLISHMENT #2:

Design your work space and production process

Tasks:

- ☐ 1. **Design your layout**
- ☐ 2. **Design your production process**
- ☐ 3. **Order/install utilities and facility improvements**
- ☐ 4. **Order furniture and equipment**
- ☐ 5. **Order inventory and/or raw materials**

1. Design your layout

Once you've found your location—but before you move in—begin to design how you'll use your space.

When thinking through your needs for office and administrative space, ask yourself the following questions:

- **What are the necessary functions of your business?** Administrative, production, shipping, etc., and how much space do you need for each?

- **Do certain functional areas need to be near other functions** (e.g., packing near shipping or bookkeeping near customer service)?

- **How will you divide the space between different functions?** Will you want permanent partitions (e.g., walls) or temporary or partial partitions?

- **How many employees will be working in each area of your space?**

- **Will you have employees working in an open environment?** If so, will you need cubicles or other ways to provide some noise abatement and privacy?

- **Do some employees need private offices?**

- **How much equipment will you have and how large is it?**

FLOOR PLAN LAYOUT

Use this grid for planning your office or production area layout. Each square is 1/8" x 1/8".
For additional grid space, use graph paper, available at any office supply store.

DESIGNING MY PRODUCTION PROCESS

As you outline the steps involved in your production process—whether you are producing a product or a service—consider the following items, how long the steps take, and who is responsible.

What supplies do I need?
When do I need them?
How much labour is required?
How will I set standards?
How will I ensure those standards are met consistently?
How will I reduce inefficiencies in the process?
How will I ensure safety?
How will I ensure adequate access to necessary utilities?
How can I reduce waste?
How will I dispose of waste?

- **Do you need conference or meeting rooms?**

- **Do you need a reception/waiting area?**

- **Have you provided space for coffee/kitchen or other break-time/ lunchtime needs?**

- **How much space is needed for storage and where is it best located?**

Don't forget to provide adequate space for all the usual business support functions—copying, faxing, mail preparation, bathrooms, and so on.

One way to design your space is to sketch a layout on a design grid, like the one provided for you on page 150. Start with a preliminary layout idea, measure your square footage, and then assign each square on the grid a measurement—one foot, ten feet, etc. Grab a pencil and start scribbling. You may want to make extra copies of the grid in case you need to start over.

Of course, you could hire an interior decorator or ergonomics specialist to help you with your floor plan, but resist spending more money than you need to now.

2. Design your production process

Your production process will vary dramatically depending on the nature of your product. The process of creating hand-made crafts is certainly far different than the process of manufacturing high-tech electronics.

Nevertheless, you still need a "process"—a plan for how you'll handle your product or service from the time an order is placed until it is finally delivered to the customer.

Even if what you're "producing" is a service rather than a tangible product, you'll benefit by considering the process by which you prepare and carry out that service.

Some aspects of designing your production process include:

- **What raw materials or inventory do you need and how will you get them? Where will you store them?**

- **What are the steps for turning those materials into finished goods? What labour is required for each step?**

OFFICE MOVE-IN CHECKLIST

✓	To Do	Notes
	Have electrical/gas wiring/piping installed	
	Order electric and gas service	
	Have telephone cabling installed	
	Order telephone service	
	Have Internet and network cabling installed	
	Set up space for server/Internet equipment, if needed	
	Order Internet service	
	Have other utility equipment installed (water, etc.)	
	Order other utilities	
	Order waste disposal service	
	Order janitorial service	
	Ensure completion of landlord's Tenant Improvements	
	Order and install interior and exterior signage	
	Have any interior exterior painting completed	
	Order and install floor coverings	
	Order and install any necessary fixtures and equipment	

- **How will you ensure quality control?**

- **How will you ship your products or goods? What shipping providers will you use?**

- **How will you pack your products? What materials will you need for packing? Where will you store your packing materials? Where will you do the packing?**

- **How will you prevent theft or loss?**

- **What kind of electricity, gas, water or other utilities do you need as part of your process?**

Use the worksheet on page 151 to address these key issues.

3. Order/install utilities and facility improvements

Hot Link

For methods and equipment to reduce energy consumption and waste, check the business information at Energy Star. **www.energystar.gov**

Once you know how you're going to use your space and have a better understanding of your production process, you can start making your space ready for your business.

One of the first things you'll want to take care of is ordering any the utilities you need: telephone, electricity, gas, Internet, water, waste disposal. It may take more than a week for the utility company to be able to install necessary wiring or turn on your service.

You will most likely need to install or adjust the wiring or location of utilities to meet your needs. While utility companies provide this service, you may also want to hire private contractors to do the work instead.

Don't forget to look at fixtures in your new space. Is there adequate overhead lighting? And what kind of signage will you need? Signs are particularly important for retail businesses.

It's easiest to make any tenant improvements—new paint, carpet, adding or moving walls, changing fixtures, etc., before you move in. If you've negotiated with the landlord that he or she will pay for any of these tenant improvements, check to make certain that the improvements will be finished in time for you to get your business underway.

Use the "Office Move-in Checklist" on the previous page for planning your move into a new space.

4. Order furniture and equipment

Few things make you feel like you're finally "in business" as much as having office furniture.

If you're just starting out, getting your stuff off the dining room table and onto your own desk reinforces the seriousness of your enterprise.

When you rent offices, how you furnish your space helps set the tone and "culture" of your company and how you'll be perceived by your staff, clients, and yourself.

Don't purchase your furniture until you know what space you'll be using. Not only do you want to make certain that your furniture fits your space, but it is possible that you may be offered furniture as part of your lease, especially in an "Executive Suite" or sublet situation.

If you expect to grow or move, look for furniture that is flexible, composed of various modules, and movable.

Remember, "furniture" consists of more than just desks and chairs— you'll need storage cabinets, work tables, floor coverings, lighting, and decorative items. Consider these as you develop your "furniture" budget.

When choosing business equipment, you may find vendors to be a good source of information and advice. For instance, if you're opening a restaurant, vendors of ovens and other kitchen equipment may be able to help you design an efficient kitchen layout.

Some of the best sources of information about industry-specific equipment are industry trade shows. Attending an industry convention or trade show is an outstanding time to compare products and prices and become more aware of the range of options available.

FURNITURE SHOPPING LIST

Furniture	Quantity	Cost per Item	Vendor	Date Ordered	Delivery Date
Desks					
Desk chairs					
Reception desk					
Guest/reception chairs					
Work/equipment tables					
Conference room tables and chairs					
Book and storage shelves/cabinets					
Filing cabinets					
Lamps/lighting					
Fire safe/security storage					
White boards					
Cubicles/space dividers					
Floor coverings					
Decorative items					
Other:					
Other:					

EQUIPMENT SHOPPING LIST

Equipment (list items)	Quantity	Cost per Item	Vendor	Date Ordered	Delivery Date

WHAT WOULD RHONDA DO?

BUY OR LEASE?

Rhonda's first rule: Purchase less expensive items; lease more costly ones. It generally doesn't make much sense to lease a fax machine or printer; they're only a few hundred pounds. But if you need a major piece of equipment, don't tie up your cash.

Rhonda's second rule: If you're uncertain about your long-term plans or needs, take short-term leases on your equipment. Even if this means making higher monthly payments in the short run, you want the flexibility of getting out of your lease if your plans change.

Rhonda's third rule: Check the tax implication of leasing versus buying: some deductions can make leasing actually cost less than buying while "expensing" purchased equipment may lower income taxes.

And Rhonda's most important rule: Don't get more than you need. Cash in the bank beats a nice desk chair any day.

When purchasing equipment, be certain you understand all the ongoing costs of owning a piece of equipment, not just the initial price. Long-term equipment costs include the cost of repairs or service contracts, the price and availability of supplies, the amount of specialised training necessary to operate it, vendor training and technical support available.

Use the Furniture Shopping List on page 156 to compare furniture and keep track of what you've ordered. Then use the worksheet on the previous page to keep track of the equipment you'll need.

Buying versus leasing: As you begin shopping, you'll be faced with deciding whether to purchase your furniture or equipment outright or to lease it instead. All kinds of things can be leased: furniture, equipment, vehicles, computers, telephone systems.

Leasing is tempting: you'll spend less money now. That frees up your capital, an important consideration for a young and likely cash-strapped company. It also may mean that you're able to upgrade or change your equipment sooner than if you make an outright purchase. In a new company, this can be desirable since your business plan is still evolving.

WARRANTIES AND SERVICE CONTRACTS

Equipment:	
Place Purchased:	
Date Purchased:	
Warranty Terms:	
Expiration Date:	
Contact Info/Phone:	

Equipment:	
Place Purchased:	
Date Purchased:	
Warranty Terms:	
Expiration Date:	
Contact Info/Phone:	

Equipment:	
Place Purchased:	
Date Purchased:	
Warranty Terms:	
Expiration Date:	
Contact Info/Phone:	

Equipment:	
Place Purchased:	
Date Purchased:	
Warranty Terms:	
Expiration Date:	
Contact Info/Phone:	

Equipment:	
Place Purchased:	
Date Purchased:	
Warranty Terms:	
Expiration Date:	
Contact Info/Phone:	

However, in the long run, you'll almost certainly end up paying much more for a piece of equipment or furniture that you've leased rather than bought outright, unless it needs regular upgrading, like a computer might.

Some vendors, especially of expensive equipment, may offer their own financing whether you're purchasing or leasing. Ask! Supplier-financed leases may be an attractive leasing option, as the vendor may make concessions on either the price of the equipment or on the financing costs to capture your business (and sell you continuing supplies or maintenance). Ask also whether this kind of financing enables you to upgrade to newer equipment during the life of the lease/loan.

Warranties/Service contracts: When shopping for equipment, evaluate the warranties, service contracts and technical support offered or available as part of the purchase. A good warranty may be worth a substantial amount of money especially if repairs are very costly. The same is true for free or low-cost technical support if the equipment is difficult to operate.

You may find that the cost of purchasing extended warranties, service contracts, or additional technical support is well worth the peace of mind you get from knowing that you won't be hit with an unexpected expense if something goes wrong.

If something does break down, how soon can you get the equipment repaired? If a piece of equipment is crucial for your business, every day lost while it's broken is lost income for you.

To help you keep track of your warranties and service contracts, use the worksheet on the previous page.

WHAT WOULD RHONDA DO?

TO KEEP WARRANTIES HANDY

We keep a "Warranty Notebook," with the warranties and instruction manuals of every piece of equipment and furniture we purchase. This is an effortless way to keep all warranties very handy and easy-to-find when necessary. Making a "Warranty Notebook" is simple—just take a thick (2") 3-ring binder and add plastic "sheet protectors." With each purchase, slip the warranty, all assembly directions, and any other instructions in its own sleeve (or more than one sleeve if necessary). We now have a few "Warranty Notebooks," of course, so we date them by year.

5. Order inventory and/or raw materials

Purchasing supplies for your business is far different from going to the mall. Your suppliers are a vital part of your company's lifeline, especially if yours is a manufacturing or retail business. You depend on having the right raw materials or inventory at the right time. In effect, your suppliers become your "partners." You are dependent on them to be able to go forward with your business.

So when you select vendors, don't just shop on the basis of price: make certain your suppliers are reliable, can maintain a shipping schedule that works well with your ongoing needs, can respond quickly if you have unusual needs, and can work with you on terms and payment.

Try not to be dependent on only one or two suppliers. If you are, you'll have less flexibility on price, and you'll be vulnerable if they experience problems in their business. If you have very specialised needs, you may be frustrated trying to find the supplies you require. Once again, industry trade shows and associations are a good place to begin.

Remember, however, that if you have very unusual requirements, you may end up dependent on only one supplier. Instead, try to design your production process so you can use more standard materials.

Use the worksheet on the next page to shop around for suppliers.

QUESTIONS TO ASK A POTENTIAL SUPPLIER

✔ How long have you been in business?

✔ What other customers do you serve in my industry?

✔ What is your usual turn-around time on orders? What is the quickest time possible in special circumstances?

✔ What payment terms do you offer? How large a credit line will you extend me?

✔ Can you meet special packing or shipping requirements?

✔ Do you have minimum order requirements? Are there discounts available?

SUPPLIER COMPARISON CHART

	Supplier One	Supplier Two	Supplier Three
Name of Supplier			
Sales Rep and Contact Info			
Range of Services/ Products Offered			
Direct Costs			
Additional Costs			
Payment Terms			
Order Turn-around-time			
Shipping Costs			
Other Maintenance/ Support			
Other:			

ACCOMPLISHMENT # 4:

Research and purchase computers, software and other technology

Tasks:

- ☐ 1. **Develop an approach to buying technology**
- ☐ 2. **Choose a phone system**
- ☐ 3. **Choose software**
- ☐ 4. **Choose hardware**
- ☐ 5. **Get online**
- ☐ 6. **Find ways to get technical help**

Technology is one part of your business you'll love and hate at the same time. Technology has enabled small companies to compete with large ones and has dramatically lowered the cost of performing many business functions. But dealing with technology can be an immense headache—decisions can be confusing and expensive to make, and difficult and expensive to change.

Whether you love technology or hate it, you've got to deal with it. You don't need to become a geek, but you've got to learn some of the basics. Just as you couldn't run a business without knowing what "accounts receivable" are, you can't run a company without being comfortable discussing Internet connections or databases.

Before you start shopping to meet your technology needs, get a good idea of what you'll be looking for. Outline your critical business needs and then look for solutions that fit those needs. Otherwise, it's easy to get enamored of "gee whiz" technology, even though you don't have a real need for it.

1. Develop an approach to buying technology

With technology changing as rapidly as it does, how do you buy something that fits your budget today yet will continue to meet your needs as your business grows and changes? Should you buy an economy model, realising you may quickly outgrow it, or should you buy the latest, fully-loaded version?

My own rule of thumb has always been to choose products I think will meet my needs and handle technology upgrades for at least two to three years. That rarely means the latest, greatest fully-loaded versions of hardware such as computers, but it also means I skip the low-end model that's about to be discontinued.

Of course, in a new company, every pound counts. That means you often have to settle for less than you'd ideally desire. Fortunately, many low-cost technology products—printers, copiers, some computers—offer excellent features that may meet your needs until your business has time to get established.

When comparing your options in choosing technology products, here are some questions to ask yourself:

- **What features do you absolutely need?** If you can't do the things you need, you've wasted money, even if you got a bargain. Consider what functions you need to perform and make certain your technology can handle those well.

- **Are your needs basic or complex?** Complicated tasks require more powerful equipment and software. For instance, tasks such as word processing, simple bookkeeping, and accessing email can be handled by the most inexpensive computers. A low-cost inkjet printer may suffice for a one or two-person office with small printing needs. But if you're creating high-end presentations you may need a more powerful computer and higher-end printers.

- **Does your new equipment have to be compatible with other equipment and software?** With stand-alone machines (such as copiers or fax machines), it may not matter if you buy an unknown brand, but with a computer or printer, you'll probably want to avoid the hassles of making an off-brand work with other equipment.

- **Do you want single purpose or multi-function equipment?** Many pieces of equipment now handle multiple functions, such as the fax/printer/copier/scanner all-in-one. These can be a good value, especially for a young company with limited demands.

WHAT WOULD RHONDA DO?

TO ORGANISE TECH "STUFF"

Every time I buy a new piece of hardware or software, it comes with a variety of disks, manuals, cords, installation guides, and more. Once it's out of the box, it's easy to get this stuff really confused with stuff from other equipment. Before long, I don't know which extra cord goes with which machine or which disk goes with which software. So I buy extra large zippable plastic bags and put each product's stuff in a bag of its own. With a permanent marker, I write the name of the software or hardware product and the date I purchased it on the outside of the bag. I then keep all these zipped plastic bags in one big box. I can easily find what I need if I ever have to reinstall something or refer back to the user manual.

- **Are replacement supplies readily available, and how much do they cost?** Especially with printers, fax machines and copiers, office and discount stores usually carry only the most well-known brands. Look at the cost of "consumables" such as ink and paper.

- **How cool do you want to be?** Ever since Apple introduced the iMac and made them in a variety of colours, the computer industry has started catching on to the importance of design. Consider design and ergonomics as you shop for technology.

2. Choose a phone system

The telephone is our single most important piece of business communication equipment. Even in this day of high-tech devices, your phone system is a key life-line to the world.

In comparison to many other forms of business communication, phone lines and phone calls are inexpensive. Compare the cost of your monthly phone calls to the cost of printing and mailing even one brochure.

Yet, a typical scenario is the entrepreneur who takes months searching for the right location, spends a bundle on a computer system, and then, at the very last minute, calls the phone company for phones. Missed calls and an inefficient phone system are the likely result.

One device in particular that most businesses need and use regularly is

MY PHONE NEEDS

	How Many?	Service Provider?	Special Features?
Voice lines			
Fax/data lines			
Voice mail boxes			
Long distance service			
Cell phones			
White Pages and Yellow Pages listings			
Other:			

Who is your local service provider? Do you have a choice in provider? _____

_____

Will you have phone numbers in remote locations? Where should they ring?_____

_____

How will you receive and direct incoming calls? Will you have a receptionist, or an automated system?_____

_____

What types of on-hold features do you need? How can you transfer calls between phone lines?_____

_____

Do you want or need caller ID, and how much does it cost?_____

Can you integrate your phone system with your database or other software? Can integration better serve your business?

_____

_____

Can you integrate your phone system with other devices, such as cell phones? Can integration better serve your business?

_____

_____

_____

the mobile phone. Mobile phones are an effective way to enable people to reach you and others—anytime. In fact, you may find that for certain employees, a mobile phone is their most important phone number, and they may not need an actual phone line at all. As you plan your phone system, consider how and whether you will use mobile phones as a supplement or a replacement for other phone lines.

Think through your phone system, keeping these pointers in mind:

- **Develop a telephone plan.** Start by sitting down and planning your phone service, just as you would any other important aspect of your business. How do you use your phones now or anticipate using them? What features must you have? How many lines do you need? How many phone lines should be wireless?

- **Consider special features.** Phone companies offer many enhancements to basic phone services. Investigate ways your phone can be a powerful business tool.

- **Keep it simple.** On the other hand, if your phones are too complicated, they'll be a nuisance to use. Phones come with a variety of features—many of which you'll rarely use. Don't buy "bells and whistles" that will get in the way of using your phone as a phone.

- **Comparison shop.** The features and costs of phone service and equipment vary widely. Shop around for long-distance plans and other services to find the right fit for your business.

- **Think long term.** Will you be expanding, moving, changing your needs? If so, either buy a scalable and changeable system, or buy an inexpensive system that you can replace without a large financial loss.

The worksheet at left will help you plan your phone system.

3. Choose software

Before you select your computers, think through your software needs—and consider them carefully. Your choice of computers can largely be driven by your software needs. If, for instance, you need powerful software programs, you'll probably need powerful computers. Also, it may be less expensive to buy your computers with programs pre-loaded than to buy them separately.

Moreover, once you've committed your business to a particular software package, it's often difficult to change, either because you can't export your data easily or because the time and effort needed to learn a new program is a barrier to making a switch.

Your most basic business functions are probably best served by "off-the-shelf," widely available software programs. An integrated office program (such as Microsoft Office or Microsoft Works), a basic book-keeping program (such as Sage for very small companies), an Internet browser, an email program, and a calendar/task program will get you started.

Another critical software need is your database. Your bookkeeping program (especially one like Sage) might serve as your database for your customer records and billing. However, you are almost certainly going to need a database to handle customer contact management, and perhaps also special needs such as tracking inventory.

If you have very specialised needs, turn to your industry association to see if there is software already developed for your type of business. Industry-specific software can be considerably more expensive than basic software, so be sure to talk with several users to find out if they're satisfied with the product.

Another approach if you have unusual needs is to have software designed or customised for your own use. However, customised software is more expensive to purchase and maintain, and if you have problems, you may not be able to find personnel to assist you.

Use the worksheet on pages 170–171 to identify your software needs and compare products as you shop for them.

4. Choose hardware

It's the rare person who gets excited about software, but it's easy to get excited about all those electronic gadgets and goodies to choose from when you look at computer hardware. Cool-looking monitors, oversize colour printers, super-sleek computers are all very tempting (until you look at the price tag, of course).

But buying hardware can also be stressful because there are so many choices, so few sources of information, and so much money on the line.

MY HARDWARE NEEDS

Use this worksheet to identify hardware you'll need in specific areas of your business.
To outline your needs for communication and software products, use the worksheets on pages 161 and 164.

	Admin/Production	Accounting	Sales	Other
Computers				
Printers				
Copiers/Fax Machines				
Other Peripherals (scanners, etc.)				
Internet Access Devices				
Network/Servers				
Data storage devices				
Cables, surge protectors, back-up generators				
Other:				

MY SOFTWARE NEEDS

Things to Consider	Office Suite	Accounting	Customer Management
What key tasks do I need to perform with the software?			
What features would be nice, but are not necessarily mandatory?			
Which program offers these features at the most reasonable price?			
What is the price?			
How simple is the product to learn and operate?			
How much free technical support is available?			
What will additional technical support cost?			
Can I find employees/ consultants who know how to use it? At what price? If not, is training available?			
Will the product integrate with my other software?			
How are the reviews and word-of-mouth about this product?			
Other:			

MY SOFTWARE NEEDS

Inventory Management	Specialty Software	Specialty Software	Specialty Software

Once again, the thing to do is to plan before you shop. Your hardware choices should be determined by your needs and your pocketbook. I've seen new companies that start with all the latest hardware before they've even developed a product or found a customer—that's not the best way to spend money. Instead, buy what you need when you need it.

Almost every business needs the basics: computers, printers, monitors, copiers, and a way to receive faxes.

For small offices, you may want to consider multi-function combination printer/fax/copier machines. These cost less than buying each machine separately and take up less room. If you are going to do a lot of printing, you may want laser printers rather than inkjet because the cost of supplies, the quality, and the speed are all higher.

As to computers, you may find it more convenient to get yourself or some employees laptops and use them both for travel and at the office.

Another thing to consider is backup equipment. You may want to invest in small backup generators that keep you up-and-running for a period of time during a black-out. You also want to find a way to backup your data daily—some solutions involve additional hardware, such as recordable CDs.

Use the worksheet on page 169 to list your hardware needs and compare hardware equipment.

5. Get online

The Internet is part of every business in the same way as phones or the mail. It's a critical way to communicate. The fact that the Internet can do so much more than just serve as a communication device may make it more challenging, but virtually every business has reason to use the Internet on a daily basis.

Internet connection: The first issue you'll face is how to connect to the Internet. The options here keep changing, so you'll want to stay abreast of the choices in your area.

To get online, you'll need an Internet Service Provider (ISP). An ISP provides you with access to the Internet, and typically, email. Most ISPs offer additional services for additional fees. Such services may include hosting your company website and registering your domain name.

COMPARISON CHART: INTERNET HOSTING COMPANIES

Use this worksheet to compare options for Internet Service Providers (ISPs).

	ISP Option One	**ISP Option Two**	**ISP Option Three**
Company Name			
Connection Speed			
Hardware Required			
Installation Cost			
Monthy/Ongoing Fees			
Services/Capacity Provided			
Website Hosting Available			
Additional Services Available			
Reviews/recommendations			
Other considerations:			

Other companies can provide additional Internet-related services, such as website design, database hosting, or writing small programs. Use the worksheet on the previous page to compare ISPs and their services.

■ **Cable or DSL:** The most common option is a "broadband" connection. This gives you faster speed in navigating websites and doesn't tie up a phone line. Faster speeds are particularly important when you go to sites with lots of graphics, databases, or animated graphics, or you use the Internet to send graphics or large files. High-speed broadband connections are available from local cable companies, phone companies, BT, Tiscali, AOL, and a variety of other providers. A choice between DSL or cable depends on the quality and price of the services available in your area. There is no consensus that one is preferable to the other.

Email: The number one use of the Internet is for sending and receiving email. Email is an all-pervasive aspect of business life. Virtually all ISPs include an email program with their Internet access, but you don't have to use the email program that comes from your ISP as your only choice. Indeed, many ISP-provided email programs are limited in their ability to handle attachments or graphics, and you may want to choose a different email program.

Most office-suite software comes with an email program. The best known is Outlook or Outlook Express from Microsoft, which come with Microsoft Office and Microsoft Works respectively. Another good choice is Eudora, which has both a free (ad-supported) and paid version.

If you travel frequently, you may want a web-based email program so you can check your email from any computer. Yahoo and Hotmail both offer free web-based email, but once again, these may be limited in how they handle attachments and graphics. And you may not want a Hotmail or Yahoo address as your business email; it doesn't give as professional an appearance as having your own domain name.

Domain name: In Week One, you learned how to reserve your own

WHAT WOULD RHONDA DO?

TO GET TECHNICAL HELP

When making a software or hardware purchase, I find out what kind of tech support is provided or available. Usually there's a limited amount of free support and a for-fee enhanced support plan. For important equipment or critical software, I always buy the additional tech support plan. That way, I have access to a person that I know has been trained on that equipment or program.

"domain name"—the name by which an Internet site is identified and located on the web. The domain name of the company that publishes this book, for instance, is PlanningShop.com. The Internet address for that domain name—or URL (universal resource locator)—is www. PlanningShop.com.

Once you have your own domain name, you can use that for your company's website address and for your email (e.g., Rhonda@PlanningShop. com). This obviously looks more professional than having a more generic email address (e.g., somebody@hotmail.com).

More importantly, you can use your domain name with virtually any ISP, website hosting company, or email program. This gives you the flexibility to shop around, use the email program that best fits your needs, and to change providers if desired.

Ask your ISP, a technical consultant, or friend how to get set up to use your own domain name with your ISP and email program.

Website: In Week Six, you will set up a company website, with an eye to how you want to market your products or services. During this week, you want to make sure you consider who will host your website as you go about choosing an ISP. After all, you may use the same company that provides you with Internet access to host your website.

It's not necessary, of course, to have one ISP provide you with both Internet access and website hosting services. However, it is frequently less expensive and less hassle to have one company do both, especially if you have modest requirements for your website.

However, if you want unique features on your website, you may want to use a company that specialises in hosting business websites. The types of features you might want to include on your site include items such as online forms for customers' to fill out, connecting your website to a database of information (such as a catalog), or to have a "shopping cart" and enable customers to purchase online at your website. Ask other entrepreneurs for recommendations of website hosting companies that they use.

QUESTIONS TO ASK — A TECHNOLOGY CONSULTANT

When selecting a consultant or technician, keep these questions handy:

✔ How long have you been in business?

✔ Do you do this full-time or is it a part-time activity?

✔ Which software programs do you have experience with?

✔ What hardware do you have experience with?

✔ Have you worked with companies in my industry before?

✔ Have you worked with companies my size before?

✔ How much do you charge?

✔ If you charge by the hour, will you give me a written estimate of how many hours my job will take?

✔ How much time do you have available?

✔ Are you available for quick help in "emergencies?"

✔ Are you available to answer tech-related questions over the phone?

✔ Do you guarantee your work?

✔ Do you have references I can contact?

You might also want to check to see if there are website hosting companies that specialise in your industry. These might have "turn-key" solutions for you that can get your website up-and-running faster than if you had someone design a website for you. They might even provide some kind of joint marketing services. Check with your industry trade association for names/listing of website service providers.

Network: You may want to build your own company internal network—a local area network, or LAN—so all your computers can work together. There are many advantages to having your own network, including the ability to share office equipment, share and store data, provide security, handle Internet access, and maintain your own internal company email.

But having a network is also more complicated than having stand-alone computers. You may need someone who is able to maintain the network. You'll also need wiring and hubs or routers to connect all the machines, and you may decide that you want a dedicated "server"—a computer whose sole purpose is to handle email, store and/or backup files from other computers, route print jobs to the office printer, etc.

Smaller and newer companies can usually get by without a network—often using the Internet itself as their network, sharing files via email.

If you aren't technologically experienced, hire an experienced company or consultant to set up your company network for you, ideally someone you can turn to on an ongoing basis for assistance. Don't depend on your brother-in-law's cousin who used to install telephones. You'll regret it.

6. Find ways to get technical help

Without a doubt, one of the most frustrating aspects of dealing with technology is the lack of capable, affordable help. Unless you have technology-proficient people on your own staff, you will be frustrated trying to find consultants or service businesses to assist you.

If you can find reliable consultants or technicians, use them. Especially when you are first getting started, use the assistance of a consultant to help you plan and install your equipment and software. Ask for recommendations, especially from other entrepreneurs, of technology consultants they've used. And make sure they speak in non-technical language that you can understand.

ACCOMPLISHMENT #5:

Consider how you will distribute your products

If you are a manufacturer, you will almost certainly use other parties to bring your product to market—distributors, wholesalers, or retailers. Choosing the right distributor and retailer for your product is vital to your success.

These intermediaries provide a variety of assistance in getting your product or service to customers, including:

- **Their sales efforts and sales team**
- **Their reputation and relationships with customers/ retailers**
- **Their expertise in understanding the market**
- **Their advertising and marketing efforts**
- **Their additional services to you—warehousing, shipping, etc.**
- **Their additional services to customers—shipping, product training or support, installation, etc.**

Distributors: Few decisions directly impact your business and your finances as much as the selection of a distributor. To a large extent, they control whether or not your products have a fair chance to ever reach potential customers. If your distributor can't get your products on retailers' store shelves, you won't be able to make sales.

Your distributor's financial practices—how long they take to pay you, how often, how they report sales, and what percentages they charge—in large part determine your cash flow and profits. And, of course, you want to make certain your distributor is honest and stable.

If you are just starting out, you may feel lucky to get any distributor to represent your product, because good distributors are in demand by many manufacturers. Nevertheless, be selective!

"Shop" for distributors, and don't choose solely on the basis of how much (what percentage) they'll charge for their services. Compare at least a few distributors. If possible, meet with a representative face-to-face. Always ask for references and check with some of the other manufacturers the distributor represents. Have their other clients been satisfied? Have they encountered problems?

DISTRIBUTION AGREEMENT

When you enter into a distribution contract, here are some considerations to negotiate.
Be certain to have any and all agreements reviewed by a competent attorney.

	Distributor One	**Distributor Two**	**Distributor Three**
Distributor Name and Contact Information			
Is the agreement exclusive or nonexclusive? What is the length of the terms, and how can either party terminate the agreement?			
What percentage do they charge? When and how often do they pay you, and what holdbacks from your payments, if any, do they make?			
What other services do they offer at what fees? What are the total fees you and the distributor are responsible for?			
Who is responsible for nonpayment by their customers?			
What minimum performance guarantees do they offer?			
What marketing efforts do they guarantee? What charges for marketing efforts do you incur or sales materials are you responsible for?			
How are damaged goods handled/paid for?			

To find a list of potential distributors, contact your industry trade association. Well-respected and known distributors are likely to be active in trade associations, and many associations maintain lists of distributors.

When entering into a distribution agreement, you should absolutely get a legally-binding contract, spelling out all the various aspects of your arrangement. Hire an attorney knowledgeable about distribution agreements to review your contract—even if the distributor says it's their "standard" contract. Some of the issues to include in your agreement are covered in the worksheet on the previous page.

Sales representatives: In many industries, independent sales representative serve many of the same functions as distributors (although they are much less likely to do warehousing or shipping of products). These independent sales reps find and call on retailers (or customers) who might want your product. However, in most cases, these independent sales representatives work for many manufacturers at once, and your products become part of the broad list of products they show potential customers.

Working with good independent sales representatives may be an excellent way to secure the services of a talented, well-connected sales force without the cost of hiring an inside sales team. However, good sales representatives are in demand, and you will have to convince them that you are worth taking on as a client.

Moreover, because independent sales representatives handle many manufacturers at once, your products can easily get overlooked in their portfolio. As a result, you need to develop and maintain a strong, ongoing relationship with your independent sales representatives. After all, you want to make certain they continually remember to include your products in their sales presentations to prospective customers.

Once again, the best place to find a list of potential sales representatives is through an industry trade association.

Retailers: Your choice of retailers, too, is critical. The retailer needs to be able to attract a sufficient number of customers, promote and merchandise your products, and then pay you in a timely fashion.

Don't be entranced by big or well-known retailers. My first client was a sportswear manufacturer who was thrilled when he landed a major department store to carry his line. Over time, however, he discovered this store had costly requirements about how he had to package and ship

RETAILER COMPARISON CHART

	Retailer One	Retailer Two	Retailer Three
Retailer's Name and Contact Information			
What discount schedule/price will they pay you?			
Are sales final or can unsold merchandise be returned?			
What are their packaging/shipping requirements, if any?			
Who is responsible for damaged goods?			
What are their payment terms/schedule?			
What promotions, advertising, or other sales efforts will they make?			
What "co-op" advertising or other promotions will you have to participate in?			
What charge-backs or other fees do they take?			
What is their reputation with other wholesalers?			
Other:			

his merchandise, and then made payments very late. And many large retailers are notoriously tough negotiators when it comes to price.

You may think that the deal you finally closed with that well-known big-box retailer is a dream come true, but once you discover how thin your profit margin will be, coupled with the retailer's strict requirements on everything from how you label your boxes to which shipping company you use, you may end up feeling that all the effort and expense of fulfilling this huge order just isn't worth it. And let's not even think about product returns

If you are selling directly to retailers (instead of using a distributor to reach them) be sure you understand all the terms of your arrangement. Who pays shipping? Will returns be permitted? Under what circumstances? What discount will they be given? How long will they have to make payments? Use the worksheet on the previous page to keep track of each retailer's specifics.

ACCOMPLISHMENT #6:
Design procedures for handling administrative tasks

Once your business is up and running, you're quickly going to find yourself having to deal with a wide variety of ongoing administrative tasks. If you don't prepare to deal with these, what inevitably happens is you soon feel overwhelmed and things start falling through the cracks.

One way to prevent this is by establishing some positive time management habits right from the start of your business and by setting up procedures to help you keep track of all the many tasks and administrative details you have to manage.

Of course, in a new business you don't yet know all of the administrative issues you're going to have to deal with. Don't worry, your administrative procedures will certainly evolve and change over time.

Nevertheless, every business—whether large or small—has to deal with many of the same administrative functions—making sure bills are paid, invoices sent out, and that things that should get done actually get done.

These can be broken down by general area of responsibility/function:

General office management:

- **answering the phones**
- **responding to emails**
- **handling incoming mail and packages**
- **preparing outgoing mail**
- **answering customer inquiries**
- **ordering supplies**
- **scheduling**
- **project management**
- **managing the "to do" list**

Bookkeeping/accounting:

- **paying bills**
- **sending invoices**
- **collecting on outstanding invoices**
- **reconciling bank statements**
- **transferring funds from accounts**
- **preparing forecasts and financial statements**
- **meeting tax deadlines and completing tax forms**

Order fulfillment:

- **order taking**
- **packing**
- **shipping**
- **tracking shipments**
- **handling customer complaints**
- **insuring sufficient supplies and inventory levels**

One way to approach these issues is to begin an "Operations Manual" detailing how you handle the tasks you perform repeatedly. As you deal with an administrative task, jot down the steps you've used to complete it. That gives you the beginning of a procedures manual, so you won't have to re-invent the process each time. Also, it will make it much easier to train employees.

Another useful approach is to create "templates" of all the forms you'll use over and over again such as invoices, statements, proposals, product/ service descriptions, etc. You can often find standard templates as part of your software programs (such as invoices, statements, and packing slips in QuickBooks) or from your industry trade association.

You can even prepare standard answers to email or phone inquiries. It's okay to use the same form over and over or to repeat yourself from one customer or client to the next. After all, you don't have to be very creative in handling these tasks.

Here are a few ways to make the most of your time and reduce administrative hassles:

- **Maintain a calendar and keep it visible:** You can use a paper calendar on your desk or on the wall, but you may find some of the features of calendar software programs (such as pop-up reminders) helpful. A good calendar feature is included in Outlook, included in Microsoft Office (not Outlook Express). Be careful, however, that you don't forget your appointments when the computer is turned off.

- **Make a "To Do" list:** Keep it somewhere where you can see it all the time. Look at it frequently and revise it daily. Check off tasks as you complete them—that gives you a sense of accomplishment.

- **Prioritise:** Often the things that are most important to your business don't have deadlines. Make sure those vital tasks are on your "to do" list and keep them on the top of the list. Don't let the pressing but unimportant details of your business keep you from attending to the truly critical.

- **Set time aside:** Make "appointments" with yourself to do important tasks and don't allow interruptions. Make certain you schedule time for sending out your invoices.

- **Reduce shopping time:** Keep a list of things you need so you reduce repeat trips. Make certain you have enough of supplies you use regularly. Order online and/or have supplies delivered.

- **Eliminate errands:** Keep a list of errands and do a number of them at one time. Schedule your errands for the end of the business day, rather than prime time. Use delivery (and pick-up) service for frequently used services (such as copy companies, shipping).

- **Use your "Vital Statistics" list**: In Week Three (page 95) you started developing a list of key company data. You're likely to be asked this information on many forms or dealing with suppliers or government agencies. Have it handy so you don't have to go digging through files.

- **Make colour-coded files:** Use files of different colours—or at least different coloured labels—so you can quickly find the kind of information you need on your desk or in your file drawers. You might want to use blue files for client project-related documents, green files for financial information, yellow files for suppliers, or whatever works for your company. Mark your files by year, so you can easily archive older files.

- **Keep frequently-used files handy:** Get a desk with at least one file drawer so you can use the files you need regularly without having to get up and go to a filing cabinet.

- **Become an email power user:** Take time to learn a few key tasks in your email program, particularly setting up folders and filters. Create your address book or email "groups" to those you'll email regularly.

- **Handle mail once:** The ideal way to manage paper is to handle incoming mail only once. In other words, as soon as you read it, deal with it. If you don't need it, throw it out. If it should be filed, file immediately. If you have to take action, do so. Of course, this isn't always possible, but get in the habit of deciding what to do with stuff as you get it.

ACCOMPLISHMENT #7:
Deal with insurance

One of the most frustrating expenses you'll incur when running a business is the money you spend on insurance. After all, you can't "see" what you're getting. If this is your first business, you'll be absolutely overwhelmed by the different types of insurance you'll need or want.

Figuring out your insurance coverage will be daunting. Guaranteed! So you'll need a good insurance agent, or two or three! Ideally, you'll find an agent who understands business insurance for companies of your size and industry. It's best if they're a "broker" who can offer you policies from a number of different companies rather than just representing one insurance company's products.

If you don't know any insurance agents, ask for referrals from other business owners or from service providers. You'll want someone whose advice you can trust because you are likely going to rely on their recommendations for the type and amount of coverage you should have.

Also, check with your industry trade association. Many trade associations offer lower-cost insurance specifically for the needs of companies such as yours. But still be cautious: just because a policy comes from a trade association doesn't necessarily mean it's best for you.

When you sit down with an insurance agent, consider three aspects:

■ **Incentive:** insurance you want because it's desired by your workers (including yourself) such as medical, dental, life insurance, retirement;

■ **Protection:** insurance in case something unexpected happens: liability, accident, fire, theft, business interruption;

■ **Legal necessity:** insurance others require—perhaps your landlord, such as fire or liability, or required by state law, such as worker's compensation if you have employees.

Health insurance is the kind of insurance most desired by your employees. When looking for health insurance, some of the things you'll want to find out:

■ **Do you have to, or want to, provide the same benefits for *all* employees**—or all of a certain class of employees (such as full-time employees)? This is likely the case, either as a result of state law or insurance company policy. That means you will get the same kind of coverage for yourself and make the same amount of financial contribution as your employees.

■ **How much of a contribution do you want to make to employees' coverage?** What percent of coverage or what amount?

■ **Do you want to pay all or part of dependents coverage?**

■ **Do you want to include domestic partners in dependent coverage?**

■ **How long of a "sabbatical" do you want to offer**—in case employees take a leave of absence from the company or medical leave?

Flexible plans allow employees to choose among benefits. Employees are given a certain amount by you, their employer. They can then each choose the benefits that are best for their individual situation. This gives your employees more flexibility and is particularly good when you have a

COMPARISON CHART: INSURANCE COVERAGE

	Option One	Option Two	Option Three
Health			
Dental			
Vision			
Life/Disability			
Worker's Compensation			
Fire			
Loss/Theft			
Business Interruption			
Malpractice (errors & omissions)			
Vehicles			
Unemployment			
Offsite equipment			
Offsite employees			
Other:			
Other:			

diverse workforce. However, there may be some financial costs in setting up or administering these cafeteria plans. Check with your accountant, attorney, or insurance agent.

Some kinds of insurance coverage—often health benefits—require you to have been in business a period of time before coverage can begin.

Always ask about the strength and honesty of your insurance provider—the company itself as well as the agent. You want to make sure the company is financially strong. After all, you need them able to cover their policies in case there's a major disaster such as an earthquake or flood.

Deciding what types and how much insurance to carry is always a juggling act. You want to have enough to cover you in case of problems, but the costs can be discouraging, especially for a young company.

Use the worksheet on the previous page to help you plan and compare your insurance needs.

week 5

DEAL WITH MONEY ISSUES
Main accomplishments:
- ✓ Deal with money matters
- ✓ Consider financing options

Make appointments with:
- ✓ Accountant
- ✓ Banker

deal with r

oney issues

MONEY, MONEY, MONEY. This week is all about dealing with the financial side of your business, from setting up your accounts to opening up a bank account to figuring out how you're going to finance your new company.

We each bring our own personal issues to the topic of money. Almost all of us are uncomfortable talking it. Money, after all, is one of the few things left in modern life we don't discuss openly with even our closest friends or family members.

In a business context, this discomfort often extends to a reluctance to deal with budgets, bookkeeping, and accounting. Most of us are intimidated by numbers. (Who, after all, really liked math class?) More often, we just find it unpleasant to think about cash flow and profit margins and, especially, debt.

Well, it's time to deal with it. You must learn to deal with money and numbers in a matter-of-fact, 'business-like' fashion. You have to look at your financial reports without imagining they're a report card of your character, discuss a raise with an employee without feeling you're under attack, and tell a client the price of your services without flinching.

ACCOMPLISHMENT #1:
Deal with money matters

Tasks:

- [ ] 1. **Meet with an accountant**
- [ ] 2. **Learn the lingo**
- [ ] 3. **Take stock of your current financial situation**
- [ ] 4. **Clean up your credit record**
- [ ] 5. **Set up your books**
- [ ] 6. **Establish your prices**
- [ ] 7. **Open a bank account**
- [ ] 8. **Consider accepting credit cards**
- [ ] 9. **Prepare simple financial forecasts**
- [ ] 10. **Learn about taxes**

Money is at the heart of every business, and understanding money—how to raise it, account for it, and manage it—is critical to business success.

Managing money is particularly important. It's not enough to just make a profit; it is certainly possible to be profitable and still not have the cash on hand to pay your bills. That's why understanding and planning cash flow is important. Likewise, it's possible to be growing a healthy business while you're not yet profitable—by planning the right kind of financing.

Setting up financial procedures right from the start of your business will help you avoid problems as you grow.

1. Meet with an accountant

As you get your business underway, you'll need the assistance of a good, small business accountant to help you in most aspects of managing your money. An accountant who understands small business issues can help you set up your accounting procedures and books, better understand any financial or tax issues you'll face, and can help you in tax planning. You'll avoid a lot of problems by getting things set up the right way right from the start. And you'll almost certainly lower your taxes too!

Believe me, a good accountant can save you more than you pay them.

Some accounting firms can also provide you with bookkeeping or bill-paying services or recommend a reputable outside bookkeeper. If your business will require lots of invoices, bills, or bookkeeping, you may want to ask about these options, especially if you don't have the funds to hire an in-house bookkeeper.

Read through this entire section before you meet with your accountant, so that you have a more thorough understanding of the issues you need to discuss.

Use the guide "Questions to Ask: An Accountant" on the next page when you meet with your accountant for the first time.

2. Learn the lingo

Once you're in business, you're going to encounter some money-related terms repeatedly. Don't be afraid to ask someone what they mean. No one expects you to understand it all.

But to make you seem less like a novice, here's a list of some frequently-used money buzzwords. Soon you'll sound like you've been discussing money for decades:

"Red ink" or "in the red." On accounting ledgers, negative numbers used to be written in red ink. So the expressions "red ink" or "in the red" refer to showing a loss.

"In the black." Positive numbers, on the other hand, were written in black ink. So if your accounts finish "in the black," you've come out with a profit.

The "bottom line." At the top of your financial statements, you list your income. You then deduct your expenses. The number you're left with on the last line of your profit and loss statement is how much money you've made—or lost. That's your company's "bottom line."

Overhead, or fixed expenses. These terms refer to the expenses you have each month, even if you don't make a sale. Fixed expenses include

QUESTIONS TO ASK

AN ACCOUNTANT

✔ What kinds of taxes will I have to pay? What are my tax deadlines?

✔ How can I reduce my taxes? Which expenses are deductible, non-deductible or have to be depreciated?

✔ What kind of bookkeeping system should I set up? How can I set up systems to reduce the possibility of theft or embezzlement?

✔ How should I pay myself—salary or draw—and what are the tax implications?

✔ Should I use the cash or accrual form of bookkeeping?

✔ Do I need to keep track of inventory? If so, what method do I use?

✔ How do I handle payroll taxes?

✔ Do I have to collect sales tax? When? From whom?

✔ What are the implications of doing business in more than one state?

✔ What kind of retirement programme can I set up and how much can I contribute each year? What kind of retirement programmes for my employees?

✔ What other accounting and tax considerations are there for my type business?

items such as rent, utilities, insurance, phone service, and administrative salaries. Your "nut" is the total amount of these fixed expenses.

Your "burn rate." This is how much money you're going through each month. This can be different than your fixed expenses, depending on what you spend on variable expenses, such as marketing, temporary help, buying new equipment, and so on.

Variable expenses. These are the costs that change depending on how many sales you make. In other words, if you run a sporting goods store, your rent is fixed no matter how many golf clubs you sell, but the amount you spend on marketing may change.

Cost of sales. This refers to what it costs you to purchase inventory to sell to others or to purchase materials to manufacture your products.

General and Administrative Expenses (G&A) or Operating Expenses:
The amount you spend to operate your business other than COGS or
sales costs. This includes all overhead expenses (such as rent, utilities),
salaries, marketing, and so on.

Turnover: Total amount of money received from sales.

Income: The amount of money received from any source. You can, for
example, have money coming in to your business from loans or as a
result of investments.

Profit: Money you have left after deducting your costs. There's gross
profit or net profit.

Gross Profit: The amount of money left after deducting the cost of
goods sold but *before* deducting general and administrative expenses.

Net Profit: The amount of money you receive after deducting the cost of
goods sold, sales costs, and operating expenses.

Net Loss: The amount of money you're in the red if, after deducting all
expenses from all revenue, you have lost money instead of having made
money. (Let's not even think about that for now…)

3. Take stock of your personal financial situation

When you start a business, you may hope to use OPM—"other people's
money"—to build your company. Be warned: you're going to have to
rely on your own money and your own credit to be the primary source
of funding—at least until you start making sales!

So as you begin to deal with your new company's finances, take stock of
your personal financial situation and monetary assets. This will help you
plan your expenditures and prepare you to meet with an accountant.

Of course, many of the most important assets for starting a business are
not financial—assets such as ambition, perseverance, willingness to work
hard, intelligence, creativity, and so on.

But, it certainly helps to also have some financial assets—such as savings
in the bank, liquid investments, home equity, or a spouse's income.

Use the worksheet at left to note your existing financial assets and the

TAKING STOCK: WHAT ARE MY EXISTING ASSETS?

	Specifics (amount, type, etc.)	How Readily Available
Financial Assets:		
Savings		
Income from other sources		
Spouse's income		
Credit lines/Credit cards		
Stocks & other liquid assets		
Stocks & other liquid assets		
Home equity		
Retirement funds		
Tangible Assets:		
Equipment		
Furniture		
Space/Location		
Business/Professional Assets:		
Marketable skills		
Specialised knowledge		
Business experience		
Certifications/Credentials		
Licenses, Memberships		
Ability to make sales		
Good customers/client relationships		
Personal Assets:		
Education/Training		
Intelligence		
Excellent communication skills		
Outstanding work habits		
Business or financial connections		
Rich relatives or friends		
Supportive family and/or friends		
Ambition & passion		
Other		

specifics of each.

Also, take note of current or upcoming financial obligations that will reduce your financial assets. This gives you a clearer picture of your overall financial situation.

Right from the start, keep track of the money you invest in your new company. There are a few reasons for this. One, you want to be certain you can take every tax deduction you're entitled to, and without records it can be a lot more difficult. Two, you want an accurate record of all expenses and source of income. And finally, you may want to treat some of this money as loans you are making to your business rather than as an investment. Ask your accountant when you meet with him or her this week about the tax implications of doing so.

4. Clean up your credit

According to a study by the Small Business Administration, personal credit cards are the number one source of financing for small companies. Expect to use your personal credit—or give personal guarantees—for many business-related purchases or credit needs.

So you're going to want to make certain you clean up your personal credit record and give yourself as much credit as possible.

This doesn't mean it's impossible to start a business if you have bad credit—not at all. But the better your credit record looks, the easier time you'll have in getting financing from suppliers, landlords, and lending sources such as banks. Even investors may check your credit report.

- **Get a credit report:** Your credit history (payments on things such as credit cards, car payments, mortgages, student loans) gets reported and recorded. You are entitled to copies of these reports. If you have been denied credit (or employment or housing) based on information in a credit report, you are permitted to get a copy of the report free for 60 days from the time of denial. Otherwise, there is a small fee to get copies of your credit reports.

  There are three major credit reporting agencies: Equifax (www.equifax.com), Experian (www.experian.com), and Trans Union (www.transunion.com). Not all credit-granting or credit-checking companies use all three, so you may want to get copies of each of them.

- **Learn your credit score:** As a result of these reports, you will be assigned a credit "score." The primary credit scoring agency is a private company, Fair Isaac (FICO). Most major financial institutions—particularly banks and mortgage lenders—use your FICO to determine how good your credit is and whether they will lend to you. So you certainly want to check your FICO score. You can do that online.

- **Make certain everything is accurate:** Read over your credit reports in detail. If there are any inaccuracies, contact the credit bureaus and the lender to correct any incorrect or outdated information. They are required to investigate within 30 days, but this doesn't mean your credit report will get cleaned up within that time, so get on top of this as fast as possible.

- **Pay your bills on time:** You want to start creating a clean credit history as soon as possible. The best way to do this is to pay your bills on time *every month*. If necessary, just pay the minimum amounts required, even if you have to maintain higher balances. Remember, you're going to need credit a year from now, so if you start paying your bills on time now, in 12 months, you'll have a much stronger credit report regardless of what it looks like now.

- **Don't increase your debt:** If your credit is really bad, cut up your credit cards and pay for everything in cash. Don't cancel your accounts—even old accounts. It's generally better to have more credit available to you than you actually use. And don't think that cutting up your cards means you don't have to pay the outstanding balances!

- **Increase your credit limits:** If your credit is good, and you handle credit well, ask for an increase in your credit limits. Now that you're in business, it may come in handy to have more funds available, especially if you need to purchase materials to fill an order or travel for business.

- **Reduce your interest rates:** You may have fairly high interest rates on some of your credit cards, especially if you've had them for some time. Call the companies and ask them to reduce your rates to be more competitive with current rates.

- **Make a list of your credit cards:** You'll find it very handy to have a master list of all your credit cards, your credit limits, interest rates and balances. That way, when you need to use a credit card, you'll know which one to choose. Since you may not be able to get business credit

MY CREDIT CARDS

Every business relies on credit cards—but some more than others. You may be relying on credit cards to help finance some of your start-up costs, such as equipment purchases. You may also need to manage your credit card debt before or after you start your business to make sure you have a clean credit report. Use this space to track credit card offers, credit cards you already have, credit card debt you need to pay off, or other useful information about your credit cards.

Name of Card Issuer	Card Number	Credit Limit	Interest Rate	Other Fees	Current Balance

for a while, designate certain credit cards to use only for business and keep those records separate.

Use the worksheet on the previous page to make a list of your credit cards and their current balances.

5. Set up your books

I'm not sure where the term "books" first came to be used for a company's accounts, but that's the basis of the term "bookkeeping." Perhaps it's because the record of a company's financials transactions were written down in a journal or book.

In fact, many small businesses still keep their books in an actual book. I did. My first set of company "books" was a simple lined ledger. On one set of pages, I wrote down my income as I received it—that gave me a picture of my total income for the year. On other pages I wrote down each time I billed a client and their payments—that gave me a record for each client. On another set of pages, I wrote down each time I spent money or paid a bill for my business—that gave me a picture of my total expenses for the year.

This was hardly the most efficient way to keep accounts, but at least I could see how much money I had made, how much each client owed me, and, at the end of the year, how much to deduct when preparing taxes. Of course, it was tedious to have to figure out how much I spent on different categories of expenses (equipment, travel, meals, office supplies, etc.) and I couldn't do any kind of "data mining" to later market or follow-up with clients. But it worked much better than nothing!

However, simple and inexpensive computer programs enable you to keep track of your company's accounts quickly, and give you a lot more power in analyzing your expenses, following up on customers, and preparing your taxes.

- **Bookkeeping software:** If yours is a very small business, you may be able to handle all your bookkeeping needs with a simple "chequebook" money-management program, such as Microsoft Money. This is designed primarily for personal record-keeping, but many small businesses use Microsoft Money and find that it's quite sufficient.

  However, it's likely that you'll need a more powerful bookkeeping program, such as Microsoft Accounting. Microsoft Accounting is downloadable free from www.msofficeaccounting.co.uk. This works for Windows users; Mac users might want to look at MYOB. Another bookkeeping program is TAS Books from Sage.

  You may also be able to find industry-specific bookkeeping programs; check with your industry association. However, be careful of getting programs that do not integrate well with other standard programs (such as Microsoft Excel). Ask your accountant what he or she uses – you may be able to save some money by sending them a file that's ready to be imported straight into their system

- **Accounting method:** One thing you'll need to determine is whether to keep your accounts on a "cash" or on an "accrual" basis. Your accountant will advise you.

  Cash basis: You enter expenses and income as they actually are paid or received. This is by far the easier method of accounting. Most small companies can keep their accounts on a cash basis.

6. Establish your prices

Figuring out how to price your products or services is certainly one of the most perplexing questions for first-time entrepreneurs or those who are new to an industry.

Here's an old joke: A shop owner purchases pencils for ten pence a piece and then sells them for nine pence. Noticing this bizarre behaviour, his partner asks, "How do you expect us to stay in business that way?" The man replies, "Volume!"

Surprisingly, many novice entrepreneurs choose a relatively similar business strategy. They imagine all that's necessary for success is to price their products or services less than the competition. Low prices, they assume, will generate sufficient sales to more than make up for smaller profits.

Competing on price alone is risky. Some discount outlets do build thriving businesses on low prices, but this strategy almost always means narrow profit margins, which in turn means less cash floating around your company. With a small financial cushion, you're vulnerable with every slight increase in costs. The landlord raises your rent 5%? That may be your entire year's profit. And you're at risk from competitors: if you become a serious threat and they have deeper cash reserves, they can just undercut your prices and wait until you're squeezed out of the market.

Moreover, customers attracted solely by price are fickle. If they shopped around a lot before choosing you, they're probably going to shop around continually. And as soon as someone has a lower price, you're history!

Of course, when you're just starting out in business, you may want to set your prices lower (even much lower) than the competition. This gives you a chance to build a customer base and get some experience. Especially if you're in a service industry, you're going to be learning a lot while working for your first customers, so it's only fair to charge them less.

In Week Two, you did some research on the prices competitors are charging (see page 66) and that should help you get an idea of the market as you establish your own prices.

Professional service fees

Setting fees is more of an art than a science when what you're selling is expertise. After all, if you're smarter than the lawyer down the street but he has more experience, should you charge less or more? What if you work faster? Why does one management consultant charge $50 an hour and another $250? Is the second really five times better than the first?

Clearly, setting professional fees is inexact. Nevertheless, there are generally-accepted practices and ranges. The two primary ways of pricing services are on an "hourly" basis or on a "project" basis.

- **Hourly:** Most professional services can be charged on an hourly fee. This rewards you appropriately when you are performing long, complicated tasks for a client. However, you may find yourself short-changed when what you are selling is your existing knowledge or expertise, and it doesn't take long to convey that to your client.

- **Project:** On a "project" or task basis, you establish a set or minimum fee for an entire project. Clients often like to pay on a project basis because they like knowing what they will be charged before they commit. Project fees reward you when your knowledge enables you to finish projects quickly but penalises you if you've badly misjudged the amount of time a given project will take.

WHAT WOULD RHONDA DO?

MONEY MANAGEMENT TIPS

- **Review your books regularly.** When you're running your business, you may not take the time to sit down and look at your financials. But you can't manage your money without having the facts. At least once a month, preferably once a week, look at your figures: accounts payable and receivable, expenses, cash flow, etc.

- **Send them your bill!** I'm always surprised by how many businesspeople, especially consultants and professional service providers, delay sending out their invoices. You may feel uncomfortable asking someone for money, afraid of being challenged on how much you've billed, or just too busy working. But the longer you wait to send out your invoices, the greater the chance you won't get paid.

- **Watch your inventory.** If you produce goods, you'll always be tempted to produce more because you get savings based on volume. But inventory can go "bad"—become out-dated, unsaleable, time- or weather-worn. Inventory doesn't just apply to finished goods for resale. You may have "inventory" in the form of marketing materials. Keep an eye on your actual use and make your purchases not only on the basis of price but whether you can get small quantities only when you actually need them.

- **Manage your growth.** You want your business to get bigger, but if you grow too fast you may not be able to sustain it. Growth costs money—you incur many expenses before you see additional income. Plan your growth so you have the financial resources to pay for it.

- **Save.** Every business has income fluctuations. The best way to have cash when you need it is to put some away when you've got it.

One way to establish fees is to determine typical fees charged by others for similar services. Contact an industry association, ideally located in your geographic area, to get a sense of typical fee structures and ranges.

In the final analysis, the appropriate fee is always the same: whatever the market will bear. Only time will help you sort that out.

Prices for goods and other services

If you are a retailer or a reseller of products or services produced by others, it's often relatively easy to figure out how much to charge. Most industries have generally-accepted mark-ups over the cost of goods (for example, 100% in department stores, 200% for jewelry).

Understanding normal practice in your industry is a good place to start when figuring how much you want to charge. Suppliers themselves will often let you know what the normal mark-up is on their goods (but be careful—there are some laws limiting suppliers from setting the final prices of their goods). Of course, you may want to price your goods more aggressively, especially in the earliest days of your business.

If you are the manufacturer or producer of goods or services sold by others, the reseller will set the final price to the end-user. They, in turn, are going to set their prices based, on large part, by what you charge them. If your costs to the reseller are too high, then they won't be able to make money and won't purchase from you. It's critical for you to know what your competitors are charging those same resellers.

Of course, you have to cover your costs and make a profit. And that's typically how manufacturers and others set prices. This is "bottom-up" planning: figure your costs for raw materials, labour, overhead, shipping, returns, etc., and then set a reasonable figure for profit.

Some brilliant businesspeople have built great companies by knowing how to maintain ultra-low prices or convince customers to pay premium prices. Most of us, however, need to stick to the normal range.

7. Open a bank account

A good relationship with a bank can be a big help to a growing company. Many people just select the bank located close to them, or the one with the lowest fees. But that doesn't mean it's the right bank for you, especially as you grow your business. Ideally, you want a bank that will work with you and your company as you grow, that will provide some understanding of your situation and allow some flexibility in dealing with you.

"Interview" a number of banks and meet their business account representatives. Develop a relationship with a good business bank while your business is still small. But expect that relationship to pay off—in terms of credit—as you get larger.

Take some time to "shop" for a bank for your business. The worksheet on the next page can help you compare banks and banking services.

8. Consider accepting credit cards

Credit cards! We like using them and so do our customers. But getting approved to accept credit cards—be a "credit card merchant"—isn't necessarily easy, especially for a new business. You will have to go through a credit check and submit financial documents, and even with excellent credit, you may still not get approved.

The first thing to do is to check with your bank to see if they can help you become a credit card merchant. They may be a bit more expensive than other credit card processors, but you may be more likely to be approved by your own bank. Be careful to avoid scam artists—your email is likely to be filled with spam offering you the chance to "accept credit cards." Beware—you're going to give them a lot of personal financial information. Only deal with a reputable company.

Accepting credit cards benefits you as well as your customers:

- **You receive payment right away.** If you bill your customers yourself, they may take 30 days or more to pay.

- **The credit card company, instead of you, generally assumes the risk of non-paying customers.**

- **You have less paperwork since you don't have to send invoices or statements.**

- **It increases the number of customers who do business with you.**

These benefits come at a cost, however. Some fees:

- **"Discount" fee.** The credit card issuer (typically a bank) takes a small

COMPARISON CHART: BANKS

	Bank Option One	Bank Option Two	Bank Option Three
Bank Name			
Location/Phone number			
Name of bank rep. handling business accounts			
Accounts offered and fees charged			
Loan or credit lines available			
Special business services offered			
Your overall impression of this bank and its services			
Other notes:			

percentage (2-4%) of every charge. This is the basic cost of administering the credit and assuming the risk, as well as marketing.

- **Transaction charge.** This is a small set amount on each transaction regardless of amount.

- **Monthly minimums you must meet.**

- **Set-up fees.**

- **Equipment purchase or leasing.**

- **Chargebacks.** This is the amount the issuer will charge any time a customer refuses payment on a charge of yours stating dissatisfaction with the product.

For instance, if the bank's discount was 2%, the transaction fee £.30 and monthly minimum £20, each $100 transaction would cost you £2.30. If you conducted ten £100 transactions in a month, the bank would make £23.00, but if you only made five transactions, the credit card issuer would only have made £11.50 (£2.30 times five), and you'd be charged another £8.50 to meet your minimum.

The manner in which you accept credit cards affects your costs. If a customer presents the card to you in person, and you can physically see and get the customer to chip and pin, you'll be charged less than if you're accepting phone, fax, mail, or Internet orders. The reasoning behind this is that there is less fraud committed when a customer has to physically present the card.

Deciding which provider to use depends on how you'll deal with credit cards. If you'll have few credit card charges, look for a low monthly minimum, even if the discount or transaction fee is somewhat higher. If you expect large transactions, shop for a low discount rate.

If you're not ever going to see or get the customer to chip and pin, you theoretically shouldn't have to pay for the credit card equipment. However, that's in theory. Many companies make you lease the equipment anyway, but don't accept that without asking.

If you and your customers are both comfortable with the Internet, one less expensive alternative is using an online credit card payment service such as Paypal (www.paypal.com). A big advantage is there's no set-up fees, monthly minimums, equipment rentals. But both you and your customer have to register online to send and/or receive payments, and if they're not already registered with Paypal, you'll have to ask them to do so. Citibank has a similar programme.

Once you decide to accept credit cards, be careful to follow the issuer's rules. Credit card companies typically have strict rules prohibiting merchants from applying extra charges for accepting credit cards.

As more and more customers—even business customers—depend on credit cards, you, too, may find yourself saying, "May I charge that?"

9. Prepare simple financial forecasts

People in business usually fall into one of two categories—those who are fascinated with numbers, and those who are frightened by them. If you're in the second category, you're probably intimidated by the very prospect of having to fill in the financial forms in this section.

Take heart. Numbers are neither magical, mysterious, nor menacing. They merely reflect decisions you have already made in your business planning process. Every decision leads to a number, but numbers themselves are not decisions. You cannot pull a number out of thin air because the financial forms call for a specific figure on a specific line.

If yours is a very small business, you may only need to prepare a simple budget: a forecast of your estimated sales and a list of how much you plan to spend on the various components of your business. Most other businesses will benefit from preparing at least simple financial forms—especially cash flow projections to help you determine or adjust your spending. And if you're seeking outside financing, you'll need a range of financial documents to give to potential lenders or investors.

Besides helping you figure out your spending, there's another reason to draw up financial forecasts—it helps you set goals. Writing down specific numbers for your anticipated sales gives you a target to work towards.

One key to good financial planning is to create your financial projections at the same time you are planning your business. If you choose to locate your business in one town versus another, there's a cost associated with that. If you exhibit at a trade show, there's a cost with that.

Budgeting strategies

Successful financial projections are achieved by budgeting from the "bottom up," not the "top down."

"Top down" numbers are enticing to work with because they always come out looking good, but they're not realistic. Here's how they work: you look at the big picture—the total market size, growth rate, average sales price, and average profit margins. You make what seem to be reasonable assumptions, something like achieving a 10% market penetration, or improving margins by 2%. Then you fill in your financial statements to make the totals come out to the big numbers projected.

For example, let's say you've invented a new golf club, and you project you will achieve a 1% market penetration within 3 years. If total annual sales of golf clubs is £2 billion, then you'll achieve £20 million in annual sales. With a profit margin of 15%, your net profit will be £3 million.

Sounds good, doesn't it? "Top down" projections result in some very impressive numbers—the kind that make you and perhaps some potential investors excited. They're just not very realistic.

Instead, the best financials are developed from the "bottom up." You do the real business-building legwork: examine different distribution channels, source manufacturers and suppliers, develop a staffing chart, outline your marketing programme, and design operations. You plug in numbers from these realistic projections of how much things will cost, and then determine how much income you need to sustain that cost.

So, let's say you're that same golf club manufacturer, and you're building your financials from the "bottom up," here's how it would work:

You first compare distribution channels, and then choose one. Let's say you decide to sell through specialty golf retailers and country clubs. This channel has associated costs and impact on income. You'll need to budget for a sales force to sell to those shops, exhibit at the annual sporting good trade shows, and advertise in "Golf Retailer" magazine. But you will only receive 40–45% of the final sales price of the club, since the retailer takes half and the salesperson receives a commission.

Now you're starting to get real numbers to plug in to each of the lines of your financial forms. You've got numbers for advertising, staffing, and income.

All this planning takes work, but there's help. The best place to start is by speaking with others in your industry, attending trade shows, and contacting your industry association.

Cash flow

If the three most important things in real estate are "location, location, location," the first three rules of business are "cash, cash, cash."

It's necessary, of course, to be profitable, but "profit" is a number that shows up on your accounts at the end of the year; cash is money you have in the bank. In a small company, it's cash that determines whether you can pay your bills.

No matter what your business is, you're going to have a lag between outgo and income. If you're a consultant, you have to pay for your phone, computer, marketing materials, and rent before you get your first client. Once you've got them, you're not going to see complete payment for at least 30–60 days after you finish a project.

Things are much worse if you're a manufacturer. You've got to pay for raw material, equipment, and employees many months before you'll see final payment.

So draw up a cash flow projection. Even if you don't write up a budget or income statement, it's a good idea to sketch out when you expect money to come in and when you need money to go out.

Use the Financial worksheets on the following pages to develop the range of financial forecasts for your business. Be certain to do the "Cash Flow Projection" worksheet on pages 218–219 to forecast your cash needs. You can find electronic versions of these worksheets at www.Planning-Shop.com/worksheets.

10. Learn about taxes

Nobody likes paying taxes, but if you're in business, you're going to have to pay them. In fact, the more successful you are, the more taxes you'll probably pay.

Understanding key tax concerns is critical for most businesses. You will make some decisions—or alter them—based on tax implications.

Some business expenses are fully deductible, others are only partially deductible, others have to be depreciated over a number of years, and others are not deductible at all. You should have at least a fair understanding of those issues as you make choices in your business.

If you purchase a very expensive piece of equipment, for instance, expecting to deduct the total cost of that from your income, you may be rudely surprised that the expense has to be spread out over as many as five to ten, even twenty years.

Tax codes are complicated and always changing. Certain tax laws apply to incorporated businesses and not unincorporated ones, or vice versa, and business tax laws differ from regulations for individuals.

So, plan on spending some time with your accountant just talking about taxes. Ask him or her to help you understand which taxes you're liable for, when your taxes are due (e.g., quarterly VAT returns and annual income tax) and how various transactions and expenses are taxed (meals and entertainment expenses, for instance, can not typically be fully deducted while other marketing expenses usually can be). Have your accountant help you plan how to reduce your tax liability.

Many businesspeople find it helpful to set up separate savings accounts just for income taxes. With each check they receive, they set aside a certain percentage in this separate tax account, so when income tax time arrives they have the money necessary to pay their bill.

As a business, you often have responsibility for collecting and then paying taxes owed by others. For instance, if you are VAT registered and standard rated, you must charge and collect the sales tax on items you sell to consumers. Set up records to keep track of those taxes that you've collected—and pay them by the dates due.

You may want to—or sometimes be required to—set up separate accounts to keep the taxes you collect distinct from your other funds. Governments, really frown on you keeping their money.

SALES PROJECTIONS

	Monthly 1st Year	Total 1st Year	Monthly 2nd Year	Total 2nd Year	Monthly 3rd Year	Total 3rd Year
Product Line 1						
Unit volume						
Price						
Gross sales						
(Commissions)						
(Returns and allowances)						
Net sales						
(Cost of sales)						
GROSS PROFIT						
Product Line 2						
Unit volume						
Price						
Gross sales						
(Commissions)						
(Returns and allowances)						
Net sales						
(Cost of goods sold)						
GROSS PROFIT						
TOTALS FOR ALL PRODUCT LINES						
Total Unit volume						
Total gross sales						
(Total commissions)						
(Total returns and allowances)						
Total Net sales						
(Total cost of goods sold)						
TOTAL GROSS PROFIT						

MARKETING BUDGET

	Monthly 1st Year	Total 1st Year	Monthly 2nd Year	Total 2nd Year	Monthly 3rd Year	Total 3rd Year
Professional Assistance						
Marketing/PR consultants						
Advertising agencies						
Direct mail specialists						
Graphic/Web design						
Brochures/Leaflets/Flyers						
Signs/Billboards						
Merchandising displays						
Sampling/Premiums						
Media advertising						
Print (newspaper, etc.)						
Television and radio						
Online						
Other media						
Phone directories						
Advertising specialties						
Direct mail						
Website						
Development/Programming						
Maintenance and hosting						
Trade shows						
Fees and setup						
Travel/Shipping						
Exhibits/Signs						
Public Relations/Materials						
Informal marketing/Networking						
Membership/Meetings						
Entertainment						
Other						
GRAND TOTAL COSTS						

PROFIT & LOSS PROJECTION

Year:	January	February	March	April	May
INCOME					
Gross Sales					
(Commissions)					
(Returns & Allowances)					
Net Sales					
(Cost of Goods)					
GROSS PROFIT					
EXPENSES - General & Administrative					
Salaries and wages					
Employee benefits					
Payroll taxes					
Professional services					
Marketing and advertising					
Rent					
Equipment rental					
Maintenance					
Depreciation					
Insurance					
Telephone service					
Utilities					
Office supplies					
Postage and shipping					
Travel					
Entertainment					
Other:					
Other:					
Other:					
TOTAL EXPENSES					
Net income before taxes					
Provision for taxes on income					
NET PROFIT					

June	July	August	September	October	November	December	TOTAL

CASH FLOW PROJECTION

Year:	January	February	March	April	May
CASH RECEIPTS					
Income from sales					
Cash sales					
Collections					
Total cash from sales					
Income from financing					
Interest income					
Loan proceeds					
Equity capital investments					
Total cash from financing					
Other cash receipts					
TOTAL CASH RECEIPTS					
CASH DISBURSEMENTS					
Inventory					
Operating expenses					
Commissions/returns & allowances					
Capital purchases					
Loan payments					
Income tax payments					
Investor dividend payments					
Owner's draw					
TOTAL CASH DISBURSEMENTS					
NET CASH FLOW					
Opening cash balance					
Cash receipts					
Cash disbursements					
ENDING CASH BALANCE					

June	July	August	September	October	November	December	TOTAL

WHAT WOULD RHONDA DO?

MANAGING PAYROLL

Soon after I hired my first full-time employee, I started using a payroll service. Determining payroll deductions and depositing payroll taxes with the proper authorities can be time-consuming and exacting. Moreover, the penalties for being late or getting things wrong can be substantial. It's much easier—and safer—to hire a professional service to take care of the administrative details of payroll for you.

A payroll service charges a modest amount, based on the number of employees, and how many states your employees are located in, but you're likely to easily save at least this amount in terms of your own administrative staff time, bookkeeper or accountant's help, and any penalties you may incur for late or inaccurate payments.

Some taxes incur substantial penalties for late or under payments, so be certain to keep track of when taxes are due and give yourself enough time to prepare them.

VAT

VAT was discussed in Week Three—see page 98 to review what VAT you'll need to collect. Then talk to your accountant this week about any questions you have about VAT.

The worksheet at right can help you keep track of your tax obligations and due dates.

ACCOMPLISHMENT # 2:
Consider financing

Tasks:

☐ 1. **Determine whose money you want**

☐ 2. **Develop a business plan**

Ask an entrepreneur starting or expanding a business to name their biggest problem, and you'll probably hear: "Where do I get the money?"

MY TAX DEADLINES

Tax	Amount	Where to Send/File	Dates Due
Income tax			
Payroll and other employment-related taxes (Social Security, National Insurance, unemployment, etc.)			
VAT			
Import/export, custom taxes and duties			
Capital gains taxes			
Inventory taxes			
Other:			

What may come as a shock is how long it will take for your business to reach a level of income where it can pay its own way. If you're dependent on your business income to support yourself or your family, you may want to consider looking for outside funding.

Just be warned: raising money is not easy and it's not fast. It's unlikely you'll be able to get financing within a six-week time frame, especially if you're seeking investors. And looking for outside money may distract you from going after the most important source of funds—making sales!

One basic difference you must know before looking for money is the difference between "debt" and "equity" financing.

- **Debt:** This is usually a loan, line of credit, or equipment financing. The money must be paid back whether or not the business flourishes. You often begin making payments on the debt soon after receiving the loan ("debt service") so you have an additional monthly expense. You give up no ownership of the company, however.

- **Equity:** This is usually referred to as getting an "investment." With equity financing, you give an investor a piece of the ownership of the company and a share of future profits and, often, a say in decision-making. But if the company fails you do not have to pay anyone back.

There are also a few forms of financing that combine the two, such as "convertible debt" in which a loan can be turned into stock. If you or your investors/lenders want to explore some of these options, consult an lawyer or accountant.

1. Determine whose money you want

Not all money is equal. When you first start looking for financing, you may be tempted to take any money you can find. Be careful. The various sources of money seek different rates of return on their loans or investments, have varying levels of sophistication and comfort with risk, and provide you with significantly different advantages and disadvantages.

Remember, you're going to have an ongoing relationship with your money source. You'll save yourself a lot of time and grief if you seek money only from sources that are right for you.

The main funding sources for starting or expanding a business are:

QUESTIONS TO ASK **POTENTIAL INVESTORS**

✔ Why are you investing in this business?

✔ What aspect of this business is most appealing to you?

✔ What other businesses have you invested in before?

✔ May I call some entrepreneurs you've invested with before?

✔ How soon do you expect to see a return on this investment?

✔ How would it affect you if you were to lose the money you're investing?

✔ If you felt I was not capable of building this company to the stage you'd like, what would you do?

✔ How do you see decisions being made? By whom?

✔ What role do you want, if any, in the company (e.g. board membership, etc.)

✔ Do you understand all the risks in making this investment?

Your own assets. Forget the old saying about using "other people's money." It's better to start or grow a business with your own money. If you have sufficient assets, particularly savings or other income that don't require you to take on additional debt, you're in the best financial position. You don't go into debt, and you don't give up equity. If your savings are owned jointly with a spouse or partner, be certain to get their acceptance and understanding of your plans.

Sales/Income. The very best way to fund a business is from sales revenues. If you can grow your company based on money received from customers, then you don't take on debt and you don't give up equity. This is not as impossible as it sounds, especially if you are starting a low-cost business. The key is to try to line up clients before you actually set up shop, and to grow only as big as your revenues permit. Your growth may be slower, and it doesn't seem as sexy as getting a huge investment, but you'll sleep better at night.

COMPARISON CHART: INVESTORS

	Investor One	Investor Two
Investor's Name		
Contact Info (email, phone, address, fax)		
What type of investor is this? (venture capitalist, angel, family, other)		
What industries do they invest in?		
What stage of companies do they invest in? (seed, startup, second round, etc.)		
What range of amount of investment do they make?		
What geographic areas do they invest in?		
What are their other criteria for investment?		
What other companies have they invested in?		
Who do I know who can help me reach this investor?		
How do they prefer to be contacted?		

Investor Three	Investor Four	Investor Five

Credit cards. Experts will tell you credit cards are a terrible way to finance a business—they cost a lot (high interest rates) and put your personal credit at risk. They're right—if you have other alternatives. The truth is most people use credit cards at one time or another to pay business expenses, particularly in the start-up phase. And credit cards can be a useful way to handle short-term cash flow problems; if you realistically expect income soon, credit cards may be an easier or better alternative than other loans or taking on an investor.

But be careful! Credit cards are generally an expensive form of financing (exceptions are low introductory rates). You can incur very high charges if you are even a day or two late on your payments. Credit card debt easily gets out of hand, and you have to pay the money back.

If you haven't already, fill out the worksheet "My Credit Cards" on page 201 to keep track of the credit cards you have.

Friends and family. Want to lose a friend? Borrow money from them or have them invest in your business. Getting family or friends involved in your business is dangerous, but there are exceptions. If the person understands your business, truly comprehends the risks, and is someone with whom you can communicate well, the situation may work. Always have loan or investment papers drawn up with the terms of the repayment or investment absolutely clear.

Banks. Realistically, banks loan money only to companies that have been in business for at least one or two years and have been successful. As your company grows, you'll likely want a line of credit from a bank to help you manage your cash flow. If you do get a bank loan for a new business, you'll almost certainly have to give a personal guarantee and have to put up personal assets as collateral. The Small Business Service provides loan guarantees to banks to encourage them to make small business loans. Business Link will be able to tell you all about current loan schemes.

Strategic partners. There may be other businesses that want you to succeed, and they may be willing to help you get underway. Perhaps they are a supplier, customer, or business serving the same market. In some cases, they may directly invest in your business or give you loans. Perhaps they would let you use their offices or equipment or otherwise help offset some of your expenses in return for the benefits you bring them.

QUESTIONS TO ASK — BEFORE YOU SEEK FINANCING

✔ Are you willing to give up some amount of ownership of your company?

✔ Are you willing to have debt that you must repay?

✔ Are you willing to risk property or other assets?

✔ How much control of the oversight of your company are you willing to relinquish?

✔ What other help do you want from a funder besides money?

✔ How fast do you want to grow?

✔ How big do you want your company to be?

✔ What do you see as the long-term relationship between you and your funding source?

"Business angels." Business angel is the term applied to private individuals who invest their own money in new companies. Because it is their own money, they often have a wider range of kinds of companies they'll invest in, and seek more diverse types of returns on their investment, than professional investors such as venture capitalists. They usually invest a smaller amount of money than professional sources. Business angels are generally much more accessible and more appropriate for small companies. A number of "business angel networks" or organisations have sprung up in large cities.

Venture capitalists. Venture capitalists are professional investors using institutional money. They generally only invest in companies needing substantial sums of money to grow very large very quickly, and will serve very large markets. They do provide early stage investments as well as financing for companies that are growing. They are particularly active in technology-related businesses. VCs have high expectations of return on their investment but are willing to take substantial risks. VCs take an active role in managing the companies they invest in, often even replacing or removing the founders from management.

Hot Link

For a list of venture capital firms see the British Venture Capital Association (**www.bvca. co.uk**) and for Business Angels see the British Business Angel Association (**www.bbaa.org.uk**). There are also regional groups of business angels such as the London Business Angels (**www.lbangels.co.uk**), Yorkshire Association of Business Angels (**www. yaba.org.uk**) - try a search engine on the Web like Google for your local group.

The comparison chart on pages 224–225 help you decide whose money you want. Consider your various financing sources, and answer the questions to find the one that suits you and your business best.

2. Develop a business plan

If you're going to seek funds from outside investors or lenders, you'll need a business plan. A business plan is a document that outlines your entire business strategy, financing, competition, staffing, future developments, and the steps necessary to achieve your results. It's different from an operating plan, which is designed primarily to help company management organise day-to-day activities. And it's different from this guide, which is designed to get you up-and-running!

The Successful Business Plan: Secrets & Strategies, leads you step-by-step through the process of developing and writing a business plan and looking for funding.

week 6

OPEN YOUR DOORS

Main accomplishments:

✓ Develop a marketing plan

✓ Set up a simple website

✓ Start making sales!

✓ Hold your grand opening

✓ Look towards the future

Make appointments with:

✓ Potential customers

✓ Key referral sources

open your

doors!

GET READY TO OPEN YOUR DOORS! This is the week when you're finally ready to start making sales. After all, the most important component in running a business—at least a successful business—is that you are able to attract and keep customers.

In earlier weeks, you've set up your business, taken care of red tape, found a location, dealt with money matters, and got your operations up-and-running. This week you'll design your marketing plan and sales strategy, centered around a clear message for your company. Then you'll go out and call on potential clients or customers—or open your doors so they can call on you. You might even hold a grand opening. Congratulations!

Develop a marketing plan

Tasks:

☐ **1. Clarify your company's message**

☐ **2. Come up with your elevator pitch**

☐ **3. Decide on your marketing vehicles**

You have to have customers to stay in business: it's the most basic business truth. Since reaching customers costs money, and money is always limited, your marketing strategy must be carefully and thoughtfully designed. That's why you need an overall marketing plan.

First, let's define the terms "marketing" and "sales" and how they differ.

Marketing is designed to increase customer awareness and deliver your message. It includes activities such as advertising, creating brochures and collateral materials, and public relations.

Marketing also includes what's called "networking"—meeting potential customers and referral sources through informal activities, such as joining organisations, attending industry events, or taking people to lunch. In smaller companies, networking may be the major marketing activity.

Sales, on the other hand, is the direct action taken to secure customer orders. The term "sales" encompasses telemarketing, sales calls, special promotions, and direct-mail solicitations.

In each of these activities—whether it's a direct sales call, an advertising campaign, or a Rotary luncheon—you want to convey a consistent, clear message about your business, and more importantly, what your product or service does for your customer: its features and benefits.

1. Clarify your company's message

Every business sends a message through its marketing. Your message is based on the strategic position your company stakes out for itself, such as "low-price leader" or "one-day service." Your message could also specify a particular market niche: "specialists in estate planning" or "software for residential architects."

Most marketing strategists agree that people buy benefits, not features. Customers are more concerned about how a purchase will affect their lives than about how the company achieves those results. No matter how cool you think your new improved business process is, your marketing message should concentrate on the benefits customers receive.

The four P's of marketing

What messages do you send customers to motivate them to purchase your product or service? Traditional marketing experts emphasise the elements known as "the Four P's," in influencing customers to buy.

1. **Product.** The tangible product or service itself.

2. **Price.** The cost advantage.

3. **Place.** The location's convenience and decor.

4. **Promotion.** The amount and nature of the marketing activities.

These elements leave a lot out of the marketing picture, however—especially as customers look for products or services not just to fill an immediate need but to enhance their overall sense of well-being.

What customers want: Rhonda's five F's

A better way to sum up what customers want is through the Five F's:

1. **Functions.** How does the product or service meet customers' concrete needs?

2. **Finances.** How will the purchase affect their overall financial situation, not just the price of the product or service, but other savings and increased productivity?

3. **Freedom.** How convenient is it to purchase and use the product or service? How will they gain more time and less worry in other aspects of their lives?

4. **Feelings.** How does the product or service make customers feel about themselves, and how does it affect and relate to their self-image? Do they like and respect the salesperson and the company?

5. **Future.** How will they deal with the product or service and company over time? Will support and service be available? How will the product or service affect their lives in the coming years, and will they have an increased sense of security about the future?

Customers, of course, would like to receive benefits in all these areas, and you should be aware of how your product or service fulfills the entire range of their needs. But your primary message must concentrate on one or two of these benefits that can effectively motivate your customers.

When you don't understand what customers want, it's tough to effectively sell your product or service.

2. Come up with your Elevator Pitch

When someone asks, "What does your company do?" you need a brief, clear answer that quickly sums up the nature of your business. This has to be short!

Here's the test for whether a marketing statement is brief enough: could you explain your business if you ran into a potential client on an elevator ride in a three story building? That's why it's called the "elevator pitch." If it takes you more than three floors to describe your company, you're saying too much.

The message must not only be short; it must be clear. Unless you're in a highly technical field, your neighbour or your grandmother should be able to understand your services well enough to describe them to someone else. If people you meet can't quickly grasp what you do, they'll never be able to do business with you or send business your way.

Every successful business has its strengths—its place in the market. So how do you get your message across?

Your elevator pitch should touch—very briefly—on the products or services you sell, what market you serve, and your competitive advantage.

If you're in an easy-to-understand business, your elevator pitch theoretically could be very short: "I sell real estate." But that doesn't distinguish you from all the other realtors out there. A more memorable elevator pitch sets you apart: "I sell homes in the Lakewood district, specialising in first-time buyers."

MY ELEVATOR PITCH

Use this worksheet to develop your elevator pitch. Remember to keep it short; focus on what customers get, not what you do; and make it easy to remember.

My Company...

Is named:
Does:
Serves this market:
Makes money by:
Is like these other companies:
Will succeed because:
Aims to achieve:

MARKETING VEHICLES COMPARISON CHART

QUESTIONS	DIRECT MAIL brochures, fliers, coupons	SIGNAGE vehicles, building, billboards	PRINT MEDIA newspapers, magazines
What market do they reach?			
How big is their reach?			
What percentage of their market is my target market?			
What is the Cost per Thousand (CPM) reached?			
What frequency will I need to be effective?			
What is the reasonable immediate response I can expect?			
How expensive is the ad to prepare?			
What are this vehicle's advantages?			
What are this vehicle's disadvantages?			
Other:			

BROADCAST MEDIA television, radio	ONLINE website design, hosting, ads	PHONE DIRECTORIES yellow pages	TRADE SHOWS	PUBLIC RELATIONS, PUBLICITY

When you can get straight to the heart of the matter with your elevator pitch, customers immediately understand your benefits. It's like the Vietnamese restaurant I used to go to; I never knew the real name, but always referred to it by the big sign out front: "Fresh, Cheap, Good."

The worksheet on page 237 helps you develop your elevator pitch. After you've written a draft or two, time yourself saying it out loud. Can you deliver it in three floors or less? If not, you've said too much.

3. Decide on marketing vehicles

Once you've clarified what you want to tell customers, you have to get that message out there. How will you reach your customers?

The methods you choose are called your "marketing vehicles." You have a variety of marketing vehicles to choose from. The best method(s) for you depends on your marketing budget, target market, product or service, and marketing message.

Create a marketing budget

The most important part of your marketing programme is that you can afford it. Every marketing vehicle costs money, so carefully plan how you intend to spend your marketing pounds. Often the best marketing vehicles are not the most obvious or the most expensive. A large ad in a specialty publication may prove far more effective and less expensive than a small one in a general newspaper.

If you spend a ton of money on a huge advertising campaign but it leaves you without the money to pay the rent or make payroll, you're going to be in hot water. So, make sure you can afford the choices you make. In devising your overall marketing programme, be sure you look for:

- **Fit.** Your marketing vehicles must reach your actual target customer and be appropriate to your image.

- **Mix.** Use more than one method so customers get exposure to you from a number of sources.

- **Repetition.** It takes many exposures before a customer becomes aware of a message.

- **Affordability.** Do these vehicles fit within your budget?

MY PRINTING NEEDS

What do you need printed professionally? What requires colour?
Use this worksheet to project how many printed materials you will need.

	Colour or B&W?	How Many Needed?	Printer	Cost per Unit	Total Cost
☐ Business cards					
☐ Brochures					
☐ Pamphlets					
☐ Fliers					
☐ Publicity photo					
☐ Advertising specialties (mugs, pens, etc.)					
☐ Signage					
☐ Vehicle signs					
☐ Uniforms, t-shirts, etc.					
☐ Other:					

The worksheets on the following pages help you choose between a variety of marketing vehicles. Several worksheets focus on specific marketing vehicles, such as printed materials, trade shows, and public relations.

The "Marketing Vehicle Comparison Chart" on pages 238–239 helps turn your message into a comprehensive marketing programme using the following techniques for getting your message to the right people:

Printed marketing material

Every company needs "stuff" to hand out. Whether you call them brochures, collateral sales material, or "leave behinds," you must have printed materials. The most important piece of printed material is your business card. Get those done right away. Use the worksheet "My Printing Needs" to plan and budget your printed materials.

Customer-based marketing

The best business is repeat business. So remind past customers you exist. Keep a mailing list, send postcards or email when you have special offers, write a newsletter, or send a note or holiday greeting. Contact past customers no less than twice a year and no more than every month. Specialty items, such as pens, mugs, or calendars, are another good way to remind customers you exist. And most importantly, ask customers for referrals!

Trade shows

Trade shows are a great way to meet potential new customers and for them to meet you. A face-to-face meeting makes doing business with you a lot more inviting, and the trade show setting makes it easy for them to ask you questions about your company.

Trade shows can be expensive—the cost of being an exhibitor, preparing your booth, printing marketing materials, and, of course, bringing enough personnel to staff the booth. But a trade show is often the best place to reach your target market.

Before choosing to exhibit, however, find out as much as you can from the show's organisers about who will be attending. Talk to exhibitors from previous years' shows to see how successful they were. Use the worksheet at right, "Trade Shows and Industry Events," to keep a list of potential trade shows to attend.

TRADE SHOWS AND INDUSTRY EVENTS

Use this worksheet to keep track of trade shows or events that you should consider attending. Under "Costs" list both the cost to attend or to exhibit and "early-bird registration." Under "Attendees" list as much specific detail about the type of people who attend as possible.

Name of show/event: _____

Sponsor: _____ Date: _____

Location: _____ Costs: _____

_____ Attendees: _____

Deadlines: _____

Notes: _____

Name of show/event: _____

Sponsor: _____ Date: _____

Location: _____ Costs: _____

_____ Attendees: _____

Deadlines: _____

Notes: _____

Name of show/event: _____

Sponsor: _____ Date: _____

Location: _____ Costs: _____

_____ Attendees: _____

Deadlines: _____

Notes: _____

Name of show/event: _____

Sponsor: _____ Date: _____

Location: _____ Costs: _____

_____ Attendees: _____

Deadlines: _____

Notes: _____

Public relations/publicity

The best publicity is often "free" publicity. Getting a story about your business in the local newspaper or on TV can be more powerful than a paid advertisement. But that's not to say that such coverage won't cost you: while you don't pay for the stories directly, it will take time and effort to get the media's attention and, in the end, you may have to hire a public relations specialist.

If you want to get a story about your business in the newspaper, a magazine, on the radio or TV, the typical way is to send a press release. Of course, it takes a lot more than just sending out a press release to get coverage, but writing up a press release is a necessary—though not sufficient—way to get media coverage.

When designing your press release, remember that most people in the media are overworked. The more you're able to make your story "easy" for them—in the sense that the details are all there—the better your chances of getting publicity.

Most importantly, of course, you've got to have something the readers, listeners, or viewers of a media outlet will find interesting. Sure, you think it's important you're opening a dry cleaning business, but why should the newspaper care? Is yours the first dry cleaning business in the city? Do you provide a genuinely unique process for cleaning clothes?

What you need is a "hook." A hook is an aspect of your story that "hooks" readers in—the thing that makes your news compelling. Some stories, of course, are naturally compelling: a closely-contested election, a hot sports contest, a really cool new consumer product. But let's face it: most of us don't have stories that are naturally gripping.

Instead, we must find an angle for reporters, showing our story is timely, amusing, informative. One way is to tie your story to outside events that generate their own publicity, such as holidays, local celebrations, sporting events, or new legislation. Reporters always need timely tie-ins.

Here are other tips to help your press release be successful:

RED TAPE ALERT! Beware! Not all marketing expenses are treated the same by HMRC. While taking an ad out in a newspaper is 100% deductible, taking a client out to lunch is not. Although business entertainment is often *the* major marketing expense for smaller companies, most meal and entertainment expenses are only 50% deductible.

- **Be creative.** Reporters are tired of seeing the same old stories. The offbeat and unusual grabs attention. Sometimes just a little "twist" on a story is enough. For instance, in advance of Earth Day, you might send out a release about how your new dry cleaning process is environmentally-friendly. If you're an accountant, you might want to send out a list of the "Ten Worst Tax Deductions" instead of the Ten Best.

- **Be visual.** Television, in particular, needs visually stimulating stories, but offering a good photo opportunity will help you make it into the newspaper, too. Find ways to make your story visual: like the pet store that holds an Easter parade with pets in Easter bonnets.

- **Work with others.** Leverage the power of other organisations to gain visibility; consider unlikely coalitions, not just similar interest groups.

- **Come up with statistics.** Media outlets love numbers. If you can provide objective, trustworthy information related to your industry or market, you've got a better chance of having the story covered. Include colourful graphic representations of the statistics if possible.

- **Be available.** No one can cover or quote you if they can't reach you. Include all your phone numbers and contact information in your press release. And don't send out a press release and then leave on vacation.

- **Follow-up.** Reporters get hundreds of press releases a week. They're not necessarily going to read yours. Make a follow-up phone call.

- **Respect deadlines.** Don't call reporters when they're "on deadline," typically late afternoon for daily journalists. Mid-morning is usually the best time.

GETTING PUBLICITY

Use this worksheet to list ideas and issues related to you and your business that can generate news stories or other free publicity for your company.

Timely stories: Tie your activities to events that generate their own publicity, such as holidays, local celebrations, or new legislation.

Creative angles: The unusual, amusing, or extraordinary always gets attention. If you can, involve celebrities.

Joint publicity opportunities: Leverage the power of other organisations to gain visibility; consider unlikely coalitions, not just similar interest groups.

Visual stories: Television, in particular, needs visually stimulating stories, but newspapers also use visually interesting photos. Avoid "BOPSA:" Bunch of People Sitting Around.

Issues on which you're the "expert:" Reporters need reliable sources they can turn to quickly. Provide trustworthy, objective information, preferably with statistics.

MEDIA CONTACTS

Keep a list of potential media contacts: reporters, editors, columnists who cover issues relating to your company.

Name: _____

Title: _____

Media outlet: _____

Areas of interest: _____

Contact info: _____

_____

Name: _____

Title: _____

Media outlet: _____

Areas of interest: _____

Contact info: _____

_____

Name: _____

Title: _____

Media outlet: _____

Areas of interest: _____

Contact info: _____

_____

Name: _____

Title: _____

Media outlet: _____

Areas of interest: _____

Contact info: _____

_____

Name: _____

Title: _____

Media outlet: _____

Areas of interest: _____

Contact info: _____

_____

Name: _____

Title: _____

Media outlet: _____

Areas of interest: _____

Contact info: _____

_____

Name: _____

Title: _____

Media outlet: _____

Areas of interest: _____

Contact info: _____

_____

Name: _____

Title: _____

Media outlet: _____

Areas of interest: _____

Contact info: _____

_____

- **Do your homework.** Get to know which media outlets (TV, radio, newspapers, Internet sites, trade publications) cover your industry or the type of story you're likely to have.

- **Develop a database of appropriate journalists, and keep in touch with them.** If possible, get to know them personally. Reporters need reliable sources they can turn to quickly.

Finally, keep trying—over and over! The companies that often get the most coverage are those that regularly and repeatedly send press releases. A one-time press release is far less likely to get you coverage than an ongoing public relations campaign.

Use the worksheets on pages 246 and 247 to keep a list of publicity opportunities and media contacts.

Advertising

Advertising works. It gets your company's name and message to a large number of people with relatively little work on your part. But it costs money. Don't buy ads based merely on the number of people they'll reach; make sure the ad reaches the *right* people: the customers you want.

A badly designed and written ad may be worse than no ad at all, so spend the time and money to develop a good one.

One of the most frequent mistakes people make when designing ads is to omit necessary details, such as the company's location, hours of operation, phone number, website. Usually the reason is that the person writing the ad takes basic information for granted. After all, you already know what city you're in or what your area code is, so you forget that it's not obvious to the reader.

Essential details:

1. **The name of your company!**

2. **The nature of your product or service.** Unless you own Marks & Spencer or Microsoft, don't assume readers automatically know what your business sells. Even if you send your ad only to existing customers, many people remember a business by what it sells—not its name. (e.g., "The drycleaners at Main and Second streets," "that cute clothing store downtown.")

3. **Where you're located.** Include the city and state (even your country if doing business internationally or online). This is critical if you're in retail, but even if your customers don't come to your store or office, including a location helps customers relate to your business.

4. **Hours and days you're open or hours and days of the sale.**

5. **Website address.**

6. **Phone number with STD code.** If you're not going to be available to answer calls, record a message with vital information. Include country code if you do business internationally.

7. **Email address.** This can be omitted if you don't answer emails.

8. **Special terms or limitations, if any.** In other words, are the discounts not applicable to certain types of items or services, or does the offer expire after a certain date?

Those are the basics. Once you've got those covered, what can you do to make your ads more effective in getting sales?

1. **Create an eye-catching headline.** The first thing you have to do is get attention. This doesn't have to be incredibly clever—"Fifty percent off" gets my attention.

2. **Tell the benefits.** Let potential customers immediately know why they should be interested in doing business with you. This can be something as simple as "Lowest Price for your Motor Insurance."

3. **Provide lots of information.** Ads chock-full of specific products are often surprisingly effective, as long as they're not too cluttered.

4. **Have a pleasing design.** This doesn't have to be the most creative or unique design, but be certain to have appropriate "white space" and don't use more than one or two type-faces.

5. **Include a call to action.** Customers often respond to a direct appeal for action, such as "Hurry—Supplies are limited," or "Call today to book your appointment!"

Finally—before you go to print, have two other people read your ad. Also keep in mind that professionals estimate it takes an average of *nine* exposures to an ad before it registers in a viewer's mind. So be prepared to run your ad repeatedly!

Promotional products

Look around your desk. How many advertisements do you have sitting at your fingertips? None? Maybe one—a clipping from the newspaper about something you're thinking of buying this week? Otherwise, most of us don't keep ads framed on our desks.

Look again. You probably have quite a few ads, you just don't think of them that way. Many of the ads you're likely to have are in the form of calendars, pens, pencils, magnets, mugs, notepads, and various gadgets—all imprinted with a company name.

These represent some of the most powerful, affordable, and overlooked forms of marketing: "specialty advertising" or "promotional products."

One of the great advantages of this kind of marketing is your customers see your name repeatedly. Studies show it takes multiple exposures to an ad before a person notices it. How many radio advertisements can you afford? Compare that to the cost of calendars or pens. If someone wants a pizza, and they have a magnet with the name of your pizza restaurant on their refrigerator, it's more likely that they're going to call you than if they look in the phone book, where they also see your competitors.

Promotional products can also make other forms of advertising more effective. Offering a free gift for new customers when you advertise in the newspaper or sending a small item in your direct mail piece can make customers pay more attention.

Interestingly, the largest percentage of promotional items sold are what the advertising specialty industry calls "wearables:" t-shirts, hats, wind-breakers, etc. Many of these are given not to customers, but to employees, either as a reward for reaching certain goals (such as safety), to promote an internal company campaign or message, or most importantly, to reinforce the company's image and logo.

To get the most of your specialty ads, keep this in mind:

1. **Target your market.** Is your audience male or female? Do they spend most of their time in the office, home, or car? Choose items your target customers will use and see repeatedly.

2. **Choose items that are useful, different, or interesting.** A lot of people get the same thing over and over.

3. **Choose a gift related to your business and appropriate for your customers.** A keychain may work for a mechanic; an accountant might want to give calculators or *big* rubbers.

4. **Simple messages are better**—you don't have a lot of space.

5. **Don't just look for price.** Customers often will keep higher quality, more thoughtful items longer, increasing the effectiveness of your promotional product.

Networking

Networking is a vital part of a company's marketing programme, especially smaller companies. Join professional or industry associations and become active. Participate in community groups. Bring business cards with you when you attend events, whether they're Chamber of Commerce meetings or assemblies at your child's school.

"Guerrilla marketing"

Finding inexpensive and unique ways to reach potential customers has become commonly referred to as "guerrilla marketing" since the term was popularised about 15 years ago.

The term reflects the concept of guerrilla warfare—using methods that are surprising, indirect, and cheap. While inexpensive advertising is not a new idea for small businesses, the idea of "guerrilla marketing" reached its peak during the dot-com boom when Internet companies spent millions of pounds on attention-grabbing campaigns.

Guerrilla marketing, however, doesn't need to be clever or outrageous to do the job. As long as the campaign carefully targets the right people and has *some* flair, it's likely to be successful. Here are some real life examples:

- When my first book, *The Successful Business Plan,* debuted, I had thousands of paper napkins printed with a humorous description of a "Business Plan on a Napkin." I attended the huge American booksellers' trade show and put stacks of these napkins on the coffee carts around the convention center hall and convention hotel bars.

- Les Schwab, a tyre dealership in the Pacific Northwest, has run a highly successful "free beef in February" promotion for 40 years. That's right—beef. Each year, they give away over $1 million of it to customers, who literally eat it up.

Hot Link

Inc.com offers tips on how to make your advertising and marketing more effective. www.inc.com/guides/marketing

■ My niece, Adeena, handled public relations for an Internet company. She printed Chinese fortune cookies with clever sayings mentioning her company. She then researched which Chinese restaurants were near the offices of the newspapers and magazines she hoped would write about her company, and gave them the cookies—free—to use whenever someone from those publications ordered Chinese food delivered.

■ A bank near my office gives free Vidalia onions away once a year to anyone who comes in. It's such a fond, and odd, local tradition that the bank gets lots of local press coverage each year.

■ Weekly, a Houston restaurant donates appetisers to a nearby motel for the hotel's afternoon guest reception. In return, the restaurant gets to put ads in each room.

As with guerrilla warfare, the problem with most guerrilla marketing campaigns is that they use a scattershot approach, hitting everything within reach. That means spending lots of time and money on things that never bring real customers. And small businesses can't afford that.

So while you might want to adopt some guerrilla marketing *techniques*, don't forget that you still need an overall, disciplined marketing *plan*.

Customer loyalty programmes

In my wallet, I have:

■ **two airlines' frequent flyer cards**
■ **a punch card from a beauty supply store**
■ **a coffee house frequent buyer card**
■ **a frequent parker card for the airport parking lot**
■ **a punch card from a car wash**
■ **three hotel chains' membership reward cards**

All these cards are evidence of my participation in these companies' customer loyalty programmes. Programmes like these have exploded over the last decade, as companies have realised the importance of retaining their customers, not just attracting new ones.

The key to creating a successful loyalty programme is being aware what you're trying to achieve. Some goals for a loyalty programme include:

- **Customer retention.** Even if customers spend no more than they would have without a programme, how much are you willing to do to keep them in your shop rather than a competitor's?

- **Maintain spending habits.** Perhaps more important than retaining a customer may be inducing them to keep their current level of spending. So you may want to reward customers for purchasing a certain number of products or spending their money with you each week/month/year.

- **Rewarding customers.** As airlines have learned, frequent user programmes can often be most effective by giving rewards to their best customers. Feeling appreciated can be a powerful tool for maintaining customer spending and loyalty.

- **Information gathering.** One benefit of loyalty programmes is finding out what your customers—individually as well as collectively—want. Grocery store loyalty programmes use this as a way of selectively marketing products based on customers' buying habits.

- **Increasing sales.** The hope is that customers will actually spend more if they feel loyal to you.

What kinds of loyalty programmes tend to be effective?

- **Buy-ahead discount.** When I purchase a pre-paid card for $20 at my nearby coffee store, I get one free drink at the time of purchase. My neighbour gets a 10% discount when she pre-purchases a series of exercise classes. The benefit is immediately apparent to the customer, and you get money in the bank now. A certain percent of pre-paid cards will be lost or never used, increasing your profit margins.

- **Free reward after reaching purchase level.** The long-term airport parking lot gives me one free day after I stay 35; I get one free car wash after buying ten. Besides encouraging me to keep coming back, I carry these cards with me—which serves as a constant ad for the business.

- **Upgrades/special treatment.** Giving extras to your loyal customers may cost relatively little but mean a lot. Some examples: an upgrade at a hotel, free dessert at a restaurant, free alterations at a clothing store.

- **Surprise rewards.** Periodically, I receive a coupon for a big discount or $10 or $25 off any purchase from companies where we do a lot of business—office supply stores, copy shops, etc. It's like getting an unexpected gift from a friend.

What kind of loyalty programmes do I find **less** effective?

- **"Percent off" discount after reaching purchase level.** Unless the discounts are substantial, these tend to feel more like a promotion for the business rather than a reward. These are different from a specific pound amount off or a specific reward free.

- **End-of-year rebates.** Waiting 12 months defers gratification too long. The customers who are likely to be motivated by such programmes are those who are most cost sensitive, not necessarily your most profitable.

No programme, though, can overcome bad service and bad products. A few years ago, I switched airlines even though I had Premier status, because I continually received rude treatment, not to mention lots of canceled flights. Treating customers like they're platinum keeps you in the gold.

Forming a virtual company

You may find that you're failing to land prospective clients because they think your company is too small or that you can't serve the scope of their needs. One way to add size, depth and strength to your company without adding even one employee is to form a "virtual company."

For instance, in a brochure for a consulting company I use, in the section, "The Team," they list an impressive group of people, each with top credentials and expertise. Looking closely, I can see that only two of these consultants are actually employed by the company. Instead, the two company founders have an *alliance* with a group of experts.

This isn't being deceptive. Below the name of each "team member" is clearly printed the name of their own individual businesses. Nevertheless, by listing these experts together as a team, they create a very positive impression; I have a full range of top specialists at my disposal.

Creating a "virtual" company—or a marketing alliance—enables you to:

- **Do joint marketing.** It's less expensive—and more effective—to combine marketing lists and create combined marketing materials. You can also reach a larger pool of potential clients.

- **Offer clients a broader range of services.** Sure, you may believe that you can serve all of your clients' needs, but the client may not feel the same way. Many clients prefer to hire specialists rather than generalists. By offering clients a team of specialists, you're more likely to get—and keep—a client's business.

- **Reduce clients' apprehension.** Many clients are reluctant to hire new businesses, one-person or very small companies. They're fearful that they could be stranded if something happens to the one key person.

- **Present a more impressive image.** Together with your partners, you're going to have a longer list of former clients, a broader range of experience, awards, and other references than you would have on your own.

One of the biggest barriers to putting together a virtual company is recognising that it's not always best to go it alone. You may have to give part of a client's business to someone else. Are you willing to get a small piece of a big pie rather than all of a very small pie—or no pie at all?

Keep in mind that virtual companies are not legal entities. There are no rules—one member of the alliance can bill the client and then subcontract with the other members, or each individual member can bill separately. The key is to stay flexible so you can meet the client's needs.

When you're looking to put together a "virtual company," look for partners that fit your own style of communication and maintain the same level of quality. And, as always, only do business with those you trust and respect.

Remember, you can't be everything to all clients, and you can't do everything yourself. As the old saying goes, "The whole is greater than the sum of its parts."

ACCOMPLISHMENT #2:
Set up a simple website

Your website is a key part of your marketing programme. Your customers and potential customers will turn to it to get information about you and your company. The first step in building a successful website is to be clear on what you want it to achieve—and make sure those goals are realistic. Many entrepreneurs suffer from the "if you build it, they will come" syndrome, imagining that if they put up a website, they'll get a flood of new customers. That's not a realistic goal.

To help you understand what you can do with a site, I've classified websites into four main types:

1. **Transactional.** This is the kind of site most retailers hope for, actually selling on the net. Perhaps the best known example is bookseller Amazon.co.uk. The problem with trying to get customers to buy on your site is that running an online store is just like running a "landbased" store: it's usually a full-time job, and you have to spend time and money getting people to your site. You also have to learn how to display and sell your merchandise on a site, just as in a real store.

2. **Promotional.** Perhaps you're dreaming your website can attract new customers from all over the world who'll find you while surfing the net. This happens in certain industries, such as travel, where customers may be willing to spend a long time sifting through sites to find a charming hotel in Paris or Istanbul. Promotional sites also work for "niche" businesses that offer a unique or hard-to-find item or service. If you're hoping to find new customers with a promotional site, ask yourself: "Will people really take the time to find a site like mine?"

3. **Informational.** One of the best uses of a website is to give information about your company to potential customers and employees who hear about you in the real world—"offline." I found a graphic designer by asking friends for recommendations, and then I checked the websites of those designers recommended. Your website can be extensive and detailed, or just include the basic information, but an informational website enables customers to find out about you, and it gives you more credibility than businesses without websites.

4. **Relational.** Finally, a website can be a good way to build closer relationships with current customers. You can post special offers, provide detailed information on topics relating to your services, and put up a FAQ list (frequently asked questions). If you have more technical capabilities, you can add forms so customers can communicate with you, track orders, or see work-in-progress.

When deciding what you're going to use your website for, keep in mind not only the initial cost of the site's design and development, but the ongoing maintenance. If your site will require frequent updates and

MY WEBSITE CHECKLIST

Use this worksheet to describe what things you want to include on your website.

✓	Website information/Features	Details/Description
	Company description	
	Products/Services description	
	Product pictures	
	Pricing	
	Contact info, address and phone number	
	Map to location	
	Portfolio/Work samples	
	Client list	
	Press clips	
	FAQ (frequently asked questions)	
	Key employee bios	
	Job opportunities	
	Reliability/Trust seals (e.g., BBB)	
	Customer bulletin boards	
	Password protected client areas	
	Password protected employee areas	
	Site map	
	Investor relations	
	Other:	

changes, you'll want to make sure the site is designed in such a way that you can easily make those changes.

Remember, most companies can succeed very well with a simple website that describes the company's services and products, basic details, and answers to most-asked questions.

Use the worksheet on the previous page to plan the functions and information you want on your website.

Website design and hosting:

In putting up your website, you basically have two options:

Hot Link
Yahoo! offers a range of website hosting services and do-it-yourself website design templates. **smallbusiness.yahoo.com/ bzinfo/prod/**

1. **Do it yourself.** Many website hosting providers offer tools to help you design your own website, including a business website, and then will host that site for you. This can be a fairly inexpensive way to get your website up-and-running. But be warned—this may not be as easy as it seems, especially if you are not tech-savvy. But if you're willing to spend some time learning the necessary skills, developing your own site may be a viable option.

2. **Get some one else to do it for you.** There's a wealth of website designers and hosting companies out there for you to choose from. But the very fact that there's so many—and the costs are so varied— makes it difficult to know which one to choose. So ask around and get recommendations from others. Certainly check with your industry or professional association; you'll probably find some developers who specialise in just your type of business. Also, ask other entrepreneurs in your community for recommendations. But don't think that hiring someone else to develop your site lets you off the hook for planning it—you'll still need to decide on exactly what you want and need, then communicate that clearly to your developer. Spend some time looking at other sites related to your industry, and then make a list of what you like and don't like. Let this help guide your planning sessions with your developer.

A general word of caution: Don't spend a ton of money on your website until you've been in business for a while. Most new companies find that they have to adjust the nature of their products or services as they encounter the realities of the market. So, don't lock yourself in to an expensive website that is likely to need changing within a year.

ACCOMPLISHMENT #3:

Start making sales!

If your marketing plan has been successful, you'll soon have potential customers interested. Now you have to make the actual sale!

Getting your first customer

While the Starship Enterprise may go "where no one else has gone before," most customers only follow where others lead. Customers prefer to patronise companies that already have other customers. What a dilemma! You have to have customers to get customers.

Don't despair; there are a number of tricks to snare that first client or customer.

The simplest method is to just give your product or service away. This isn't as stupid as it sounds. Technology companies often give potential customers "beta" or test versions of their software. They use this as a way both to improve their product and to expose future buyers to what they make. And Post-It Notes™ never caught on until 3M gave away thousands of samples. You, too, can allow potential customers to sample your products or services or to serve as "beta" testers.

Another approach is to charge your early clients far less than they would be able to get elsewhere (and less than you'll charge later). This enables you to start building a reputation and perhaps creates some word-of-mouth advertising. Lots of companies use "introductory pricing" for their products or services to start to build market share.

Another way to find your first customer is to ask your competitors for excess work they can't handle. Yes, I said "competitors." One of the biggest mistakes I made when I started was that I avoided talking to others in my field. I figured they would view me as a threat, and the less they knew about me, the better. I was wrong. It turned out my "competitors" were great sources for new business and industry information. Competitors may be interested in subcontracting or referring work to you.

If you can do so legally, or if you're on good terms with your former employer, see if there are customers you can take from your last job. Some of the most successful small businesses are those that serve customers that bigger businesses no longer wish to handle.

MY SALES PITCH

Use this worksheet to develop your sales pitch. Know your strengths and be able to explain those quickly. Under "My Pitch," list the key strengths that distinguish you from your competition. Then, anticipate objections prospective customers might raise under "Their Objections." Finally, prepare a "Rejoinder" that counters the objection and convinces your prospect to buy.

My Pitch	Their Objections	My Rejoinder

Successful sales techniques

If you're going to be in business, sooner or later you have to make sales. Some entrepreneurs view the prospect of a sales call with the same sense of fear and loathing as having to face a tax or VAT inspection.

Take heart: sales is a craft, not an art. It can be learned. Here are a few keys to successful sales:

- **Listen.** No sales skill is more important than the ability to listen. A great salesperson hears what the customer wants—their concerns and priorities. When calling on a customer, it's tempting to immediately launch in to a sales pitch, especially if you're nervous. But by listening, you can better understand how your product or service meets the customer's needs and desires. If a woman shopping for a car says she likes to drive fast, tell her about performance instead of cup holders. If a man is concerned about safety, focus on the airbags and anti-lock brakes. Don't just tell the customer what you think they'll be interested in or stick to your standard sales patter.

- **Ask questions.** You can't listen to a customer unless you get them talking. Ask relevant questions to draw them out, "What do you like in your current car?" "What don't you like?" "What features are the most important?" Don't just ask questions to qualify them as a hot prospect, such as, "Are you ready to buy a car today?"

- **Tell them what they get, not what you do.** You work with your product or service every day, so it's natural to focus on details of your work. But customers don't want to know the ins-and-outs of your business; they want to know how you meet their needs.

- **Appreciate the benefits of your product or service.** Genuine enthusiasm is contagious. If you truly believe you're offering the customer something worthwhile, you'll be a more effective salesperson. On the other hand, if you don't believe in your product, you shouldn't be selling it.

- **Don't oversell.** It's tempting to land a sale by telling the customer anything they want to hear, but that's almost certain to lead to customers being dissatisfied or disappointed. An acquaintance of mine who owns a successful chain of moderately-priced hotels told me that his strategy is to "promise customers a Chevy, then deliver a Cadillac." By under-promising and over-delivering, he has built an exceptionally loyal customer base and generates terrific word-of-mouth marketing.

- **Be Honest.** Lying is not only unethical and possibly illegal; it's a sure-fire way to lose customers and potential customers. You may even find yourself facing a lawsuit.

- **Compare, don't criticise, your competition.** Yes, I know, your product or service is *so* much better than your competitor's, and they're really not very nice people either. But disparaging your competition makes you appear malicious. Instead, factually—and positively—compare your benefits and value with your competitor.

- **Build relationships.** One of Rhonda's Rules is "people do business with other people." We all prefer to do business with people we like and trust. Consider the "lifetime value" of a customer, not just a one-time sale. Often, you might want to make a little less profit to begin an ongoing customer relationship. Get to know your customers; find out about their businesses or families. One way small businesses can compete with the big guys is by building strong customer relationships.

Your sales pitch

Most people wrongly believe a good salesperson is someone who can talk well. That's only half of it. It's equally important—perhaps even more important—to be able to listen well. By listening to customers, you find out which issues are important to them in making a purchasing decision.

At some point, though, you will need to make the pitch—actually ask a "prospect," a prospective customer, to buy your product or service.

A sales pitch can come in many forms, but it has three distinct stages:

- **Your pitch**
- **The customer's concerns and objections**
- **Your rejoinder, or reply, to those concerns and objections**

After you've been in business for a while, you'll know the objections or concerns that keep most prospects from making the decision to buy. Work on those, so you sound confident in responding to them should they arise in the course of a sales call.

It's generally best to anticipate objections and respond to them before they're even raised. This way, you can address whatever shortcomings or problems the prospect may be thinking about but doesn't want to mention out loud.

WHAT WOULD RHONDA DO?

AT A BUSINESS LUNCH

Many people take prospective customers to lunch (or breakfast or dinner) to try and make a sale. But, how, exactly, can you make the most of that opportunity with a prospect? Most inexperienced lunchers believe the main purpose of a business lunch is either to: a) conduct business, or b) eat lunch, and they're unsure how to mix the two.

Don't worry! Business lunches aren't about either business or lunch; they're about building relationships. Here are the keys to a successful business lunch:

Listen. Listen to what the other person cares about, what makes him or her tick. Many of us, when we're nervous, tend to talk a lot. Instead, let your guest do the talking. Ask questions. You don't want to conduct an interview, but you'd be surprised how smart people think you are if you ask questions and listen to their replies.

Go for no reason. Don't make the lunch seem like a sales call. Instead, ask for an informal get-together: "I'm starting a new business, and perhaps I can take you to lunch and pick your brain for some advice." Or, "I'm often in your area, how about having lunch some time?" Once you've taken the time to get to know your guest, setting up a sales call in the future will be easier.

Order slow food. Preferably, have the other person suggest a place to eat. If you have a limited budget, you choose a nice, mid-priced restaurant. Forget McDonald's. Don't be in a rush. Order "slow food," not "fast food." You want as much time with your guest as possible.

Don't order messy food. Pass on the spaghetti, and be careful about piling chili on the burger. Forget the 'three-martini' business lunch. It's wisest not to drink any alcoholic beverage at lunch, and only do so if your companion orders one first. No matter what your companion does, stick to an absolute one-drink limit. This, after all, is still business.

Turn off your cell phone. Stay focused on your companion—you've taken the time to arrange a lunch meeting, so don't waste it away on phone calls with others. It sends the message that you aren't really interested them. Your goal is to listen and learn from your guest.

Bring your credit card or sufficient cash. If you did the inviting, pick up the tab, even if your guest says, "I can put this on my company's credit card." But don't have a scene arguing over the check. You can just say, "You can get the next one." Some companies have policies that don't permit employees to be treated; in that case, split the tab.

Good luck and bon appetit!

Use the worksheet "My Sales Pitch" on page 260 to outline the points you'll make to prospective customers and how you'll handle their reservations and objections.

Feeling at ease making presentations

"I'd rather have a root canal," my friend replied when I asked if she'd rather go to the dentist or give a speech. She's not alone. Most people list speaking in public as one of their greatest fears. But if you're in many types of businesses, you're going to have to make presentations—often sales presentations—and have the attention focused on you.

Whether you're introducing yourself to 15 other entrepreneurs at a Chamber of Commerce meeting, or describing your product to 300 potential customers at a trade conference, being comfortable in front of people is a competitive advantage. When you're at ease, listeners pay more attention to your message.

The single biggest aid to increasing your comfort level when eyes are turned in your direction is to accept yourself just as you are. We all have aspects of ourselves we wish we could change. For one person it's weight, for someone else it's a receding hairline, for another it's a slight stammer that kicks in only when they're nervous. It's important to remember that *everyone* worries about their little "flaws"—it's part of being human. But it's our imperfections that makes each of us distinctive, unique, and real. Learn to accept and even cherish that which makes you different, and you'll go a long way towards being a more confident speaker.

Nevertheless, learning to accept yourself as you are is probably a long-term project, and it's not much help if you've got a sales presentation to give next Thursday. So here are a few tips to help you get over the jitters when standing in front of people:

- **Prepare.** If you're making an important sales call, learn everything you can about the prospect's company, needs, worries, market, experience with other suppliers, etc., so that you're not "flying blind." Your audience will be impressed that you've taken the time to learn about them and their needs. The same tip applies if you're making a presentation to a large group, perhaps your industry association—the more you know about who they are, the more credible you'll sound to them and feel about yourself. You've heard it before: knowledge is power—and it can make you *feel* powerful, too!

- **Practice.** Run through your pitch or presentation in front of friends or family. Have them ask questions, so you can practice coming up with answers on the fly. Even if your presentation doesn't justify developing a formal script, you'll want to have an outline on hand to make sure you cover all the important points. Also, rehearse the key phrases, explanations, examples, statistics, anecdotes, etc., that you'll want to draw upon, so they'll roll off your tongue with ease.

- **Wear something that gives you confidence.** Whether it's a new outfit or your favourite tie, you'll feel more relaxed if you think your clothes are appropriate and make you look good. New clothes can give you a sense of pride, but I know businesspeople who have one great suit or dress they've had for years and always wear for initial meetings or presentations. Make sure your clothes are clean and neat; you can hardly be relaxed if you think everyone's staring at the spot on your shirt.

- **Wear or carry something that makes you feel terrific.** There's terrific power in knowing that you're wearing the special watch your favourite uncle gave you, or the "lucky" shoes that have seen you through other anxiety-generating events. These "tokens" are more than superstition; they remind you you're someone special.

- **Concentrate on what you're good at.** Remind yourself of the special talents or knowledge you bring, and let your confidence grow from those. You'll look and act more assured.

- **Stop looking in the mirror.** It's normal to check yourself before you meet with people, but there's a limit. If you've made certain your hair is neat, make-up fixed, and fly zipped, don't take "just one more look".

- **Bring visuals.** If you're nervous when people look at you, bring lots of visual materials to distract attention. While the audience is staring at your colourful charts, they won't be looking at your face. Completely petrified before you have to make a presentation in front of a group? Okay, then prepare a Powerpoint presentation, so most of the time you're in a dark room.

- **Pay attention to others.** You'll make yourself more appealing by paying attention to your audience. Interact with them, ask questions, make eye contact, smile. Think complimentary thoughts even if you don't speak them out loud ("What a nice group," "She seems friendly.") When you think well of others, you give off a welcoming glow.

You may never get used to standing up in front of others, but it doesn't have to feel as bad as dental surgery. Just organise your thoughts, put on a nice outfit, smile, and you'll be getting rave reviews.

One-page sales sheet

When a prospective customer asks for information about one of your products or services, you'll find it useful—and easy—to develop a one-page product or service sales sheet. You'll find many uses for a one-page sales sheet: trade shows, leave-behinds for sales appointments, packing inserts, and to send in response to phone or email requests.

To give you an idea of what a one-page sales sheet looks like, take a look at one we frequently use (at right). Here's how to make your own:

1. **First, write up your text.** Keep in mind one of Rhonda's Rules: "People don't read." So keep your copy short, snappy, and to the point. Start with a one-paragraph description of your product or service. Provide the basics: what it is, what it does, and why your customer should buy it.

   Focus on your product's benefits, not just its features. In other words, think of your product/service from your readers' point of view—you may be thrilled that you just bought a brand new high-end photocopier for your print shop, but what does that mean for me, your customer? Better quality? Cheaper copies? Faster service?

   Use bullet points to list key features and benefits. Use powerful, descriptive—but true—adjectives.

2. **Next, you need a photo of your product.** Or a graphic. Or anything visual. In this case, a picture really is worth a thousand words. If your product or service isn't particularly photogenic, use a chart or graph that illustrates benefits or cost savings.

3. **If it's appropriate, include the price of your product.** In some cases, your prices may vary by customer or season, so you'll want to maintain a separate price list.

4. **Finally, you'll want a call to action.** Tell people where and how they can order your product or get further information.

Now, it's time to take all this copy and put it on the page. Here are secrets professional designers use to make print materials look polished:

1. **Divide your page into columns.** Short spans of text are easier to read and more visually appealing than long lines. Divide your letter-sized sheet into columns.

2. **Leave "white space."** Text and graphics "pop" when they have some breathing room. At the very least, make sure you have at least one-half inch margin on all four sides of your sheet and leave one-quarter inch space between columns and other graphics. It's better to eliminate some text than cram in too much.

3. **Use a maximum of two typefaces.** Your computer is loaded with wonderful, fun fonts; save most for your kids' school projects. For text, use a serif font (with those tiny lines—or feet—at the ends of letters; the text you are reading now is set in a serif font) and for headlines and captions, use a sans serif font (without the decorative lines, such as the font we used for the first sentence in this paragraph). Times Roman is a good serif choice and Arial is a popular sans serif font. Serif fonts are easier to read; sans serif look cleaner and more modern.

4. **Use colour and bold face type sparingly.** While you may want to make a few key words or phrases jump off the page by using colours or fat type, if you try to make everything pop out, nothing will.

There! You'll have a sophisticated, effective one-page sales sheet you can proudly distribute to potential customers.

Responding to prospective customers

Your phone rings. It's a prospective customer wanting information about your services, requesting a bid or proposal. That's a good thing, right?

Well, yes and no. Obviously, it's great to have potential customers knocking on your door. But not all prospects are going to convert to paying customers—no matter how good your sales skills, how competitive your prices, or how outstanding the quality of your products or services. The sad truth is you can waste a lot of precious time and money answering inquiries and preparing bids or proposals for prospects who are not ready to buy or just plain browsers.

Figuring out how much time and energy to spend on prospective customers is a delicate and difficult balancing act. You need to spend enough time to make a sale to a genuine prospect, but you don't want to waste too much time on those who won't ever buy.

Realistically, you have to be responsive to all potential customers. But there are ways to limit the amount of time, money, and effort you spend on dead-end shoppers. Here's how:

1. **Have general information prepared and available, such as your one-page sales sheet.** Most prospects will try to figure out whether a company is a good fit for them before taking up too much of their—or your—time. Let's say you sell and install floor tiles. Do you specialise in commercial or residential? Do you only serve a specific geographic area? Do you install counter tops as well as floors? That kind of information enables prospects to weed themselves out before calling you. Of course, a great and relatively inexpensive way to provide this information is on your website.

2. **Ask questions of the prospect.** In professional salesperson terms, this is called "qualifying" the prospect. By asking a few simple, non-intrusive questions, you can get a much better sense of how serious the prospect is. Some questions to ask:

   - **What's the scope of the project?**
   - **What's the timeframe for the work to be started and completed?**
   - **How soon will you be making a decision on a vendor?**
   - **How many bids are you getting?**
   - **What other alternatives (not competitors) are you considering? (In the floor tile example, for instance, the question might be phrased such as "What other types of floor coverings are you looking at?"**
   - **What are the most important considerations in your decision— price, quality, convenience?**

   Questions such as those give you a much better sense of whether a prospect is ready to make a decision, whether they're likely to find you a good choice, and how much time to spend with them.

3. **Don't get star-struck.** It's easy to get excited if you're approached by a large or well-known company or customer. Don't lose your judgment. Such customers often take up more of your time, take longer to make decisions, and expect highly competitive bids. Sure, it would be nice to have the biggest company in town or the star of the major league baseball team on your customer list, but is it worth it if you don't make a profit?

4. **Give prospects a reason to make a decision sooner rather than later.** It's human nature to put off making choices until the last minute, but that often puts your business in a crunch. If you can, come up with realistic, positive ways to encourage customers to make a decision quickly—"I've got an opening in my calendar in two weeks but then I'm booked for a few more weeks" or, "I can get a discount on materials this month only."

5. **Be cautious of prospects who want *too* much information.** Some prospects use proposals as a way of getting free consulting services. This is true of both small customers and Fortune 500 companies.

6. **Don't count your chickens before they hatch.** It's easy to get excited about a prospect, especially if it's a big one. So, keep a lot of balls in the air, and remember, a deal is not a deal until the check clears.

Finding sales leads

Before you can make a sale, you need someone to sell to. How are you going to find potential customers?

Sure, if a prospective customer walks in your door or calls, it's relatively easy to make a sale. It's much harder to find those who haven't called but have the potential to become customers—in other words, sales leads.

Your sales leads are a natural outgrowth of defining your target market (see Week Two). The better you've defined your target, the easier it will be for you to hone in on your most likely prospects. If you manufacture plumbing fixtures, for instance, you'll be far more effective in finding sales leads if you know whether your primary target is new construction or remodels, residential or commercial, contractors or consumers.

So where can you find good leads for your company?

- **Entrepreneurs' groups.** Most new and smaller companies get their first sales leads by joining organisations. There are numerous kinds of local entrepreneur groups: chambers of commerce, women's or ethnic group's business organisations, leads/referral clubs, etc. Typically, these groups set aside time at meetings for members to network, or even give direct sales pitches. Most entrepreneurs' organisations make available members' directories, and you are allowed to use that list for leads. Some groups hold "table top" mini-trade shows. To make your membership effective, attend regularly, even volunteer to serve on committees.

■ **Trade associations.** These groups are similar to entrepreneurs' organisations, but they are formed around one particular industry. You'll find local chapters of many national trade associations in most large or mid-size cities. It's a mistake to view others in your industry solely as "competitors." They can be a good source of referrals, as well as providing information and advice. In addition to joining an association in your own industry, consider joining associations of industries that you sell to or serve. Often, as a member of an association, you are given a list of other members that you can then use as a source of sales leads. Some trade associations sell their membership lists, but typically only other members are given access to this valuable resource.

■ **Trade shows.** Trade shows reach a large number of targeted prospects in a short period of time. But one additional benefit of being an exhibitor at a trade show is that you are often given (or are allowed to purchase) a list of attendees. These lists can be incredibly valuable in giving you a source of highly targeted sales leads.

■ **Newspapers.** One of the very best sources of information about your community, and thus potential customers, is your local newspaper. A real estate agent in Miami I know relies on the obituaries for leads: he solicits surviving family members of people who've died (without spouses) to see if they want to sell the deceased's home. Yes, I know it sounds ghoulish, but it works for him.

You don't have to be so morbid; try checking other parts of the paper such as:

- **public notices or advertisements about new businesses or business name changes**
- **stories about new or expanding businesses**
- **business sections of daily newspapers or business journals for listings of companies, such as largest employers**
- **wedding or birth announcements**
- **help wanted ads**
- **general advertisements and classified listings**

■ **Phone books.** Don't forget the good old-fashioned Yellow Pages. If you've identified particular types of businesses as potential customers, you can find a local list just by letting your fingers do the walking. Of course, unsolicited telephone calls aren't the most productive way to get new business!

- **Public records.** Many for-profit companies compile and sell lists of public records that might be used for sales leads. These include new business licenses or incorporations, building permits, wedding licenses and birth certificates.

- **List brokers.** Private companies sell lists of both businesses and consumers, sorted virtually every conceivable way. You can buy targeted lists of leads by industry, magazines subscribed to, products purchased, schools attended, age, hobbies, even lists of new mothers. I've never bought leads from a private broker, but my recommendation would be to make certain you've very clearly targeted your prospects, and that the list is new and continually updated. Then be sure to track your results so you know whether the list was effective or not.

Cold calling

A "cold" call is a sales call—either on the phone or in person—when the person you're calling hasn't previously indicated any interest in your products or services. Obviously it's tough to make cold calls because you're going to get a lot—and I mean a lot—of rejection.

It's not easy to make (or get) cold calls. Who hasn't been deluged with telemarketers for long distance service calling during dinner or credit card companies interrupting the work day repeatedly? But have you ever stopped and wondered why they keep calling when we all hate them? Here's the dirty little secret: cold calls work.

What's the secret of cold call success?

- **Change your perspective.** Most of us start out thinking that making a sales call is "bothering" the other person. But if you are offering something you truly believe will meet a real need at a good value, then you're not a bother but a help. My company changed payroll services based on a cold call. We were having problems with our old service, and got a cold call from a reputable firm. The new payroll service solved a problem for us—so the call was a genuine help not a bother.

- **"Qualify" your leads.** We all really *hate* sales calls when they don't relate to us. So find reasonable ways to narrow down your target list. That saves you time and increases your success rate. What makes a qualified lead? A person or business that is *likely* to need your product or service *now*.

Hot Links
One source of sales lead lists is Dun and Bradstreet, **www.dnb.co.uk**

- **Give yourself a quota.** When my younger sister—who's been a top-notch salesperson for 20 years—started out, she gave herself a quota every day. She put 20 business cards in her pocket and couldn't go home until she gave out all 20 or made a big sale.

- **Come up with a great pitch.** Be clear about what you're offering. Write out your pitch and the most important points well before you make your first call, but don't read it! Introduce yourself right at the beginning of the call. Think about the objections you're likely to hear and have responses ready. You're not going to get it right the first time—or the second or the third. So constantly practice your pitch and refine it.

- **Mind your manners.** If you walk in on someone and they're on the phone, wait until they're free. If you're phoning, and the person says "Now's not a good time," ask when a good time would be to call back, and get off the phone.

- **Take people literally.** If a prospect says, "I'm not interested right now," believe they mean right *now*. Perhaps they'll be interested another time. My sister called on a company for seven years before they finally bought from her.

- **Don't be obnoxious.** Take no for an answer. If someone's not interested, why waste your time or theirs? Be polite.

- **Stay in practice.** Cold calling is difficult, and it's easy to forget how to do it well. So make calls from time to time—it reminds you what you're offering your customers.

Finally, don't take it personally and don't get discouraged. You've got to kiss a lot of frogs before you find a prince. It took me four years of calling on the business editor at Gannett News Service before I finally got my nationally-syndicated column. And I'm still friends with him!

Up-selling and cross-selling

Getting customers isn't cheap. It takes money and time to attract new customers. Perhaps you advertise, send direct mail, attend trade shows. You put a lot of effort into getting each customer to walk through your door, call you on the phone, or visit your website, and it costs you the same amount of money whether that customer then spends $1 or $1,000. So it's far more profitable if you can make a bigger sale to each customer who comes your way.

An example of "up-selling" occurred when I went to a neighbourhood beauty supply shop. I was looking for a new eye shadow, and I went straight for what I wanted. One eye shadow—$8. Then, the nice saleswoman came over and advised me—in a very low-key manner—of a much better deal. They had a special: for $25, I could get three eye shadows of my choice, two lipsticks, one nail polish, and a cosmetic carrying case. That seemed to be a lot better deal, and by the time I left, I had a selection of beauty supplies and a $25 charge on my credit card.

When upselling is done properly, the customer gets a good deal and you get a bigger sale. How could the retailer afford this kind of offer? Because their big expense is tied up in their overhead—rent, salaries, advertising—not in the cost of the eye shadow.

Many retailers try to up-sell their customers. If you've ever been to a warehouse discount store, you'll see that many items are packaged in multiples—I can only buy two bottles of Hershey's chocolate syrup—or in sets, such as selling three related books together. The result is that the customer makes a bigger total purchase on each visit, and it's much more profitable for the retailer.

Up-selling doesn't just occur in retail. If you need to get a will drawn up, don't be surprised if your lawyer offers you a complete estate planning package, which includes a few other documents you should properly prepare at the same time. The one price package is a good value to you and a better sale for them.

A slightly different approach is "cross-selling"—selling related products or services. Examples of cross-selling include a diaper service that also sells baby care products, a travel agent who books recreation activities as well as airline reservations, a computer hardware firm that sells software.

One of the best ways to make more money from each customer is to look for ways to get continuing income rather than just making a one-time sale. Are there products or services your customers use up or use repeatedly—"consumables"—you can appropriately sell? There's often more money in consumables than in the original product or service. Decades ago, Kodak figured out there was more profit in the film than the camera. The same is true today with inkjet printers.

Service businesses, too, can look for ongoing revenue streams. Accountants frequently offer bookkeeping or bill-paying services—instead of

RED TAPE ALERT! While up-selling and cross-selling are legal sales techniques, "bait-and-switch" methods are illegal in most states and under some federal laws. "Bait-and-switch" is the practice of using an advertisement or promotion to lure a customer (the "bait") but when the customer requests the promoted item, the salesperson tells them that it is not available or inappropriate for their needs and suggests a more expensive option (the "switch"). If you use a low-cost promotion to bring in customers, make certain you have reasonable quantities available and be careful not to be too aggressive in suggesting other, more expensive products instead.

doing clients' income tax returns once a year, they work for them all year long. What could you offer your customers on a continuing or consumable basis?

Of course, there's a risk that if you're too aggressive when you upsell, cross-sell, or offer consumables that a customer will view you as too pushy and they'll leave. Remember we're a relatively conservative society as consumers and people tend to assume anyone selling anything is trying to pull a fast one. As long as you're not, you should be OK.

If you can honestly provide a more complete product or service or a better value by up-selling or cross-selling, both you and your customer will benefit.

ACCOMPLISHMENT #4:
Hold your grand opening

Now comes the big day. You're ready to "officially" open your business. It's time for a grand opening!

Grand openings aren't just for retail businesses. You can hold an "Open House" at your new office space, a "Launch Party" for even a home-based or virtual business (have it at a restaurant or other rented or borrowed space) or a "Product Launch" event for a new product or service.

While your grand opening is certainly a celebration of all the work, time, thought, and money you've put in your new business, it's primarily a marketing event. Draw up an invitation list of all those you want to know about your business, even if you know they won't attend the party or are located out-of-town. This should include potential customers, suppliers, friends, business reporters, trade association or community organisation leaders—and of course your family and employees' families.

Print up an invitation that not only lists the time, date, and place of the grand opening but also describes what your business does. Remember, this is a chance to let the world know about your business, not just invite them to a party.

Follow up with an email. The least intrusive marketing material you can send someone is an invitation to a party. After all, you're not trying to sell them anything—not yet, at least!

To top it off, write up a press release announcing your new business and send it to the business reporters of your local newspaper and any industry publications. Call them to follow up and ask them to attend. They probably won't, but you'll let them know you exist and make it easier to pitch future stories to them.

And don't forget to take a moment to appreciate all that you've accomplished. You should be proud of yourself.

ACCOMPLISHMENT #5:
Look towards the future

You've come a long way! Think about where you were when you first purchased this book—and look at where you are now. Wow! What a transformation!

I wish I could tell you that it's all downhill from here, that now you can sit back, a tall glass of lemonade in your hand, and watch the cash roll in. Unfortunately, that's just not the case…at least not yet. Certainly, getting a business up and running is one of the most difficult periods for an entrepreneur. But if you're like most businesses, the next year or two will continue to be a significant challenge for you.

You'll be spending a lot of time in the coming months looking for and serving customers, streamlining operations, figuring out which products or services are actually profitable and which are underperforming, reworking your financial projections to better align them with the reality of your business and market, worrying about cash, and keeping yourself energised, motivated, and confident about the choices you've made.

You're probably going to have some sleepless nights, questioning your ability to make the business work, worrying about details, customers, products, and mistakes. You may find that the tenuous support you initially had from family members wavers as some things don't work out as you planned. In fact, there may times that you want to ditch the whole business, heed your father-in-law's advice, and "go get a real job."

If so, congratulations! You are a perfectly normal entrepreneur! In fact, self-doubt isn't just a normal feeling that comes with starting a business, it's a necessary one. Many successful business owners are perfectly willing to admit that fear of failure is one of their single biggest motivators.

While it's true that you need to be self-confident about what you're doing, you also need to be able to analyze your choices, learn from your mistakes, and be honest with yourself about how you can change, adapt, and grow. Don't let your negative thoughts paralyze you—instead, harness that energy towards a positive purpose. In other words, turn those self-doubting thoughts into positive actions that will help you move forward. Fear, when used as a catalyst for positive action, is a good thing!

Part of helping yourself overcome fears of failure and getting through difficult times is recognising that what you are doing is worthwhile and important. Instead of seeing yourself as a struggling self-employee, recognise that you're the leader of a new but growing enterprise.

Feeling like the C.E.O.

Here's a quiz: When you meet someone new, what's the second question you're most likely to be asked? Answer: "What do you do?" This question is not asked just to figure out whether you're a welder or a writer—it's to determine how important you are. For the self-employed, that question can be tough on the ego.

Most of us associate status with our jobs. We feel good about having a fancy office or an important job title. Even if ours is an entry-level job, if we work with a big company, we often feel a sense of reflected status ("I'm a bottle-washer at IBM.")

So when you go from employee to entrepreneur, giving up those trappings of status and success can be tough.

Even good things can make you feel awkward: wearing very casual clothes everyday, going to your child's school performance in the middle of the day, not having to report to anyone. When you've been used to suits or supervisors, not having external recognition can be unsettling.

Even more frustrating—though you'll get over it—is that when you make a lot of money, often no one knows how well you're doing. After all, you still work at home and wear jeans. I had worked for myself for seven years before my friends took me seriously. What changed their impression? I got my first overseas client. Trust me: when someone pays you to go to Australia, you suddenly get respect.

But I knew I was serious long before that. Although I had given up a job where I had a private office, two assistants, and an expense account, I didn't miss any of that (well, maybe the expense account). Part of the reason is that early on, I realised I had to take some steps to make me feel good about being self-employed.

I set up a part of my living room as my "office," printed up business cards and stationery, and changed the way I answered my phone (from "Hello," to "Rhonda Abrams speaking"). More importantly, I found a symbol to remind me of my importance.

For me, it was flowers. My first couple of years in business, I didn't have much money and every penny counted. I lived on cheap spaghetti I bought in bulk. But every week, I bought flowers for my desk. Somehow, looking at a bouquet made me feel like I'd arrived at a "real" office.

Little things matter. You can't afford the assistant, you won't necessarily have a separate room for your office, and believe me, when you travel, you're going to fly economy instead of business class. See what kind of symbols help you feel good about being in business day-in and day-out. Here are a few you might try:

- **Business cards.** Absolutely! You can't exist without them.

- **Get dressed every day.** No, of course, I didn't think you were going to work nude. But how about getting out of those shell suits?

- **Set up an "office" and decorate it.**

- **Get a gadget.** Hey, many of us judge ourselves by our toys. Having a cell phone, a Palm, a cool computer can make you feel you've arrived.

■ **Give yourself a title.** You really can grow up to be President!

When is it time to grow?

I know it's hard to think about growing your business when you've just opened your doors. But if you've done most of the things in this book—and have a little luck—pretty soon you'll find yourself dealing with the issue of growth.

Most entrepreneurs hope one day their small business will get bigger, but how do you know when it's time for your business to expand? Even if customers are beating a path to your door, you must make an active choice to hire employees, add locations, extend product lines. What makes the decision more difficult is that growth rarely occurs in a straight line; you can go along for years with a healthy one-person, or twenty-person business, when suddenly business booms, and you're faced with choosing how to handle it.

You'll begin to get the itch to grow when you:

■ **Have more work than you can handle**
■ **Need to add products, services, or locations to retain your current customer base**
■ **Want to take your business in new directions without ending your current activities**
■ **See a significant opportunity in the market**
■ **Want to or need to substantially increase your income**

Perhaps the hardest step is deciding to hire your first employee. It took me almost a decade before I hired my first full-time permanent employee. I'm sorry now that I waited so long, but having an employee represents a huge change in how you do your day-to-day work, and like many entrepreneurs, I was reluctant to have both the responsibility and another person underfoot.

The next critical juncture is when your company reaches roughly ten employees. At this point, many customers may not have direct contact with you. This can make you very nervous or it may be liberating. Not all businesses can make the transition—many service businesses depend on the abilities or charisma of the founder, so expansion stops when they're no longer immediately involved.

Around 20 employees, you'll face another major turning point. This is the stage where you can no longer supervise or regularly interact with all employees, and you need managers. Many entrepreneurs consciously choose to stop their growth at this point because they want to run an enterprise where they know and manage everyone who works for them.

The final transformation from small company to big business comes at approximately 100 employees. This is when a company needs substantial outside financing to expand. Do you really want to be a public company, maintain high bank debt, or have outside investors? These choices greatly reduce your ability to control your own company but enable you to compete in much larger arenas.

With any growth comes a transition period in which you have to redefine your own job responsibilities and learn to delegate more authority to other people.

You may want to keep your business to a one-person shop or grow to hundreds of employees. Who knows?

You've given yourself—and your business—a great foundation. From that solid foundation, you can build a future of excitement, opportunity, and success.

Go for it. You can make your dreams a reality. After all, look how far you've come in just six weeks.

Index

A

Accountant, meeting with 190
ACT 44
Administration 178–181
Advertising 27, 115, 244
    cooperative 71
Advisory committee 102
Apple Computer 35

B

"Buy/Sell" agreement 22
Bank account 202
Benefits, employee 116, 117
Board of Directors 87, 102–103
Bonuses, employee 116
Bookkeeping 106, 198
Brand 27, 31
Budgeting 25, 41, 206–215
Bundling 71
Business angels 227
Business buddies 104
Business cards 27, 39
Business concept 3, 5–26, 14, 15, 16
Business description 16, 17
Business expenses 45
Business goals 16
Business idea 12
Business licenses 41, 90–92
Buisness Link 25–26, 55, 83, 222
Business lunch 259
Business name 3, 28, 34, 38
Business plan 25, 224
Business values 9, 10, 16

C

Cash flow 208
Census 55, 60
Certifications 92
Chambers of commerce 72, 75
Coca-Cola 36
Cold calling 267
Colour 26–27, 39–40
Companies House 55
Company identity 3, 26–39
Company name 30. See business name
Competition 62–67
Computers 159–173
Contact management system 43
Contracts 96
Copyrights 40, 98
Corporate culture 16
Corporation 87

Credit, personal 195
Credit cards
    accepting 203
    financing with 222
Credit score 196
Cross-selling 269
Customers 57, 59, 60, 66
    responding to 263
    loyalty programmes 248
    profile 58

D

Dataquest 56
Design 35–36, 37–40
Distribution 15, 174–178
    agreements 71, 96
Domain name 26, 28, 30, 34, 171
Dun & Bradstreet 55, 66, 267

E

Elevator pitch 72, 232
Email 160, 170
Employees 103, 107, 109–116
    benefits 110
    compensation 115–116
    hiring 112
Employee stock ownership plan 24
Employment contracts 96
Employment laws 109
Equipment 151, 153
Estate agent 131
Eudora 44
Exit plan 22

F

Facilities 127–156
Family 24
FICO 196
Fictitious business name 94
Files 41, 43
File folder labels 42
Finances, forecasting 206
Financial goals 16
Financing 22, 216–224
Forrester 56
Forum for Women Entrepreneurs 75
Four P's 231
Furniture 151–156

G

"Guerrilla marketing" 247
General Partnership 84
Getting organized 41–45

Goals 4, 6–7, 9, 12, 18, 22, 118
Google 54, 56, 66, 76
Graphic designer 26, 27, 39
Growth, managing 274

H

Hardware, computer 164
Health insurance 111
HMRC 94, 107, 241
Home office 135–144
    deductions 139

I

Identification numbers 90, 92
Identity 3, 26–39
Independent contractors 106
Industry 50–56, 72
Industry association 51, 72–73
Insurance 181–184
Intellectual property 96, 99
Internet Service Provider 168
Investments 25, 108
Investors 21–22, 23, 86–87

L

Law 21, 31 See Legal
Lawyer 41, 82
Layout, production space 145
Leadership skills 119
Lease 96, 128–129
    terminology 131
Legal 21, 24, 81, 82–99
    agreements 96
Legal form 83, 85
Letter of agreement 82, 96
Liability 84, 87
Licenses See Business licenses
Licensing 71, 82–99
Limited Liability Company (LLC) 84
Limited Liability Partnership 84, 86
Loans 25
Location 126–155
Logo 26–27, 35

M

Management 117–120
Manufacturing space 129, 130
Market 12, 15, 18, 59
Marketing 35, 41, 106
    budget 236
    material 238
    plan 230–251
    vehicles 236

McDonald's 35
Mentors 100
Microsoft
 Accounting 199
 Excel 199
 Money 199
 Office 170
 Outlook 44, 170
 Works 170
Mobile office 143–144
MYOB 199

N

Name 27, 31, 40. *See* business name
National Association of Women's
 Business Owners 75
National archives 55
National statistics 55
Networking 3, 72–76, 247
Network, computer 173
Network Solutions 34
Nike 35
Non-compete Agreements 98
Non-disclosure Agreements 97
Non-profit corporation 86

O

Office 126–155
Opening for business 270–271
Order fulfillment 68
Organizations 74
Outsource 106
Ownership 20, 86, 87

P

Packaging 38
Paid holidays 112
Pantone Matching System 39
Partners 9, 18, 21, 22, 23, 87
Partnerships 18–21, 22, 86
Partnership agreement 21
Patents 99

Paypal 205
Payroll management 106
Permits 90
Personnel 100–120
 policies 109, 110–111
Phone system 136, 161
Planning for the future 271–275
Presentations, making 260
Pricing 65–67, 199–202
Production process 145–157
Profit sharing 116
Project proposals 96
Promotional products 246
Publicity 240–244

R

Recruiting 113
Red tape 79, 82
Renting space 127–135
Research 25, 50, 52, 56, 159–173
 sources 55
Retail space 129, 130
Retirement 111
Role models 11–12

S

Salary 115
Sales 255–270
 leads 265
 pitch 258
 sheet 262
 techniques 257
Servicemarks 31, 32, 102
Shareholders 88
Shipping 149
Software 159–173
 bookkeeping 198
Sole proprietorship 85, 86
Statistics 60
Stock 87–90, 116
Straplines 27, 37
Strategic partners 71, 72, 222

Strategic position 17
Suppliers 68–69
Support structure 100

T

Target market 39, 40, 56–61
Taxes 21, 24, 82, 208 *See also* VAT
Tax id number 44, 92
Team 100–120
Technology 159–173
Telephone 161–163
Terminology, finances 191
Trademarks 26, 28, 30, 31–34, 97
Trade associations 69, 73
Trade secrets 97
Trade shows 238, 239
Training 25, 111, 117

U

UK Intellectual Property Office 33
Up-selling 268
URL 34
Utilities 150

V

Values 9, 18
VAT 82, 94–95, 209, 216, 217
Venture capitalists 223, 224
Virtual company 250
Vision 5, 7

W

Warehouse space 130
Warranties 156
Website 27, 34, 35, 39, 171, 251–254
 design 106
Work-for-hire agreements 96
Work hours 112, 141

Y

Yahoo! 54, 69